D0171734

TOUGH COOKIES

Simon Wright was formerly the editor of the AA Restaurant Guide and now works as a free-lance writer and restaurant consultant (a role which he also performed on the Channel Four series *Ramsay's Kitchen Nightmares*). He is also a partner in the Carmarthenshire pub restaurant *Y Polyn* which since opening in January 2005 has won a number of awards (including an Egon Ronay Star, a Good Food Guide entry, a place in the BBC *Olive* magazine's top thirty UK gastropubs and a listing by *The Times* in both their top ten new restaurant openings of 2005 and their top ten places for Sunday lunch) none of which he can legitimately claim much credit for. Nevertheless he can often be found there, sometimes behind the bar and regularly in front of it, but he is seldom spotted doing anything useful in the kitchen.

TOUGH COOKIES

Tales of obsession, toil and tenacity from Britain's culinary heavyweights

Simon Wright

PROFILE BOOKS

This paperback edition published in 2006

First published in Great Britain in 2005 by
PROFILE BOOKS LTD
3A Exmouth House
Pine Street
Exmouth Market
London EC1R 0JH
www.profilebooks.com

Copyright © Simon Wright, 2005, 2006

10 9 8 7 6 5 4 3 2 1

Typeset in Garamond 3 by MacGuru Ltd
info@macguru.org.uk
Printed and bound in Great Britain by
Bookmarque Ltd, Croydon, Surrey

Photographs by Adrian Franklin

The moral right of the author has been asserted.All rights reserved. Without limiting the
rights under copyright reserved above, no part of this publication may be reproduced,
stored or introduced into a retrieval system, or transmitted, in any form or by any means
(electronic, mechanical, photocopying, recording or otherwise), without the prior written
permission of both the copyright owner and the publisher of this book.

A CIP catalogue record for this book is available from the British Library.

ISBN-10 1 86197 975 4
ISBN-13 978 1 86197 975 9

To the memory of Jenny Willmott –
a Tough Cookie ahead of her time.

Contents

PREFACE

Pig Leaves Pastry Cart

It is not the critic who counts; not the man who points out how the strong man stumbles, or where the doer of deeds could have done them better. The credit belongs to the man who is actually in the arena, whose face is marred by dust and sweat and blood, who strives valiantly; who errs and comes short again and again; because there is no effort without error and shortcomings; but who does actually strive to do the deed; who knows the great enthusiasm, the great devotion, who spends himself in a worthy cause, who at the best knows in the end the triumph of high achievement and who at the worst, if he fails, at least he fails while daring greatly. So that his place shall never be with those cold and timid souls who know neither victory nor defeat.

Theodore Roosevelt (1858–1919), 'Man in the Arena' speech, 23 April 1910

I used to edit a restaurant guide, let me in from the cold.

You see, I never did feel quite warm enough in the critic's clothes. Although I could throw on a pretty cloak of credibility (having done time as a restaurateur always helped), there were occasions when it seemed a threadbare and transparent garment. When a chef asked (as they often did), 'What the hell do you know about it anyway?' that seemed to me to be a reasonable question that deserved an answer. After all, they'd done all the work, I'd just sat on my ever expanding backside and eaten the results. 'Critics are like pigs at the pastry cart,' John Updike once said – food critics are especially so.

It wasn't that I was doubtful of my ability to distinguish good food (more of that later in the book), but I was less convinced of my right to do it. Having run a restaurant, or more accurately been part of the running of a restaurant, I had a good idea of what was involved and in particular what was going on in the kitchen. It's no picnic.

That little bit of insight that I'd had was good for me, humility-wise; it helped me to take the job seriously. I knew how hard it could be on the inside and so sitting on the outside, making judgements, I felt I had to exercise a certain amount of responsibility. As a restaurateur I'd had limited affection for critics. On the whole we didn't have much to complain about. Being way out in West Wales meant that we were rarely on the radar anyway and our reviews tended to be limited to the *Good Food Guide*, which was always friendly enough, and the odd bit of attention from the Welsh press. That was until I received a tip-off from a friend who ran a car rental firm in town telling me that there was a guy on his way to us who had just picked up a hire car rented for him by a national paper. He might be a reviewer, he thought.

Judging by the number of questions the man asked me during his dinner, it seemed my source wasn't far wrong. Frankly, if I hadn't been forewarned, I could probably have worked it out for myself. The anonymity of the restaurant critic can be a charade of theatrical magnitude. Lone diners in restaurants aren't that common, lone diners in the countryside are as rare as red squirrels, lone diners who ask that many questions, take notes and request a copy of the menu may as well have 'critic' tattooed across their forehead. But of course, all this goes unsaid. Instead the evening turns into something between a ballet and a farce with reviewer and reviewed dancing around each other and exchanging furtive glances, both completely aware of the ritual being played out but both nevertheless keeping up the pretence. Simple words become imbued with extraordinary weight. Put yourself in the critic's seat. You've finished a course and the host comes across personally to clear the plate. 'Did you enjoy that, sir?'

How the hell can you answer that, especially if you didn't? If you do the easy thing and say yes, you envisage a spontaneous party breaking out in the kitchen, followed by weeks of eager anticipation as they wait for the review to appear. Then you shiver to imagine the vitriol directed at you when they read it and it's less than glowing. 'The bastard! He even said he enjoyed it, the two-faced, fat, four-eyed … etc., etc.' Restaurant reviewing does little for the karma.

I don't recall whether this particular individual commented on the merits of his meal on the night. He seemed happy enough, and when a couple of weeks later we received a call from the paper with a request for more menus, we were quick to oblige. As well as the current one, I sent a copy of the new menu that was to start shortly. The article would appear in the following Saturday's paper.

I was out of the house at 6.30 a.m. and in the paper shop ten minutes later. As soon as I'd shut the car door behind me I began scrambling through the various sections until I found the write-up. The first impression was that it was okay, not great but okay. I read it again. He'd said some nice things but he'd also heavily criticised a couple of dishes – the pasta starter in particular was condemned as dull. Driving home deflated, I thought of how the girls were going to take being censured in a national newspaper. They'd begun making the fresh pasta only a couple of weeks back and it was proving a bit of a hit with the customers, but not it seemed with this critic.

Then it struck me. *He didn't eat the pasta.* The pasta wasn't even on the menu at that point. In fact, although he'd dined alone, the review commented on a meal for two people; half of it was based on dishes that hadn't been sampled but were on the new menu I'd sent to the paper. Disappointment turned to indignation. Here were the three of us struggling to make a living running a restaurant in rural West Wales and some critic from London writes a fault-finding review about us in a national paper based on an experience that he never actually had. Fuelled by rage, I fired off an intemperate letter to the editor of the paper explaining the injustice of it all. That night a few of our customers mentioned that they'd seen the piece. They were as indignant as I was, but it didn't help much. I just wished the whole thing had never happened.

A few days later I received replies from both the editor and the critic himself. The editor expressed his complete faith in his writer, the critic claimed he could tell the dishes were dull from just reading about them. If that was the case it seemed odd to me that he was bothering to visit restaurants at all. Why not just ask them to send you a menu and save yourself all that bother and expense? I thought about saying as much but the anger had subsided by then and anyway we had a restaurant to run.

About a month later I picked up a trade magazine with a lead story on a hotel restaurant in South Devon. They'd had a restaurant critic visit and he'd written an unfavourable review in a national newspaper. The chef, dejected, had handed in his notice. The dishes the critic condemned weren't the ones he'd eaten – it was the same paper, it was the same critic. I called the owner in South Devon, told him I'd seen the piece and related our own experience to him. Had I also seen the story in *Private Eye*? There was a piece about it in there too. I bought the magazine and sure enough there it was; the *Eye* had contacted the paper's editor suggesting that the reviewer should be sacked but the editor was still standing by his man. My fury reawakened I wrote to the *Eye* with our own tale and they printed it in the next issue. It must have been the final straw, and at the end of the story they reported that when they'd brought this second incident to the attention of the paper, the critic had been sacked.

A victory of sorts. It was a reckless and cavalier way to behave, but despite that I can't say I felt wonderful about the guy losing his job and many years later I still don't. Like I said, restaurant reviewing does little for the karma.

☆ ☆ ☆

Let's be real, the guide I edited, the *AA Restaurant Guide*, is not the most influential food guide in the country. Among chefs, recognition from Michelin is the ultimate goal, among the public the *Good Food Guide* is more widely read. I doubt that even a microscopic fraction of 1 per cent of the population could name the handful of five rosette restaurants in the 2003 edition of the AA guide. Of the tiny number who could, I would guess almost all of them are chefs. And this is the great anomaly about guidebooks. Even the best-selling have a limited impact upon public perception, and on the whole, a change in somebody's rating is unlikely to have a huge impact on business, but, boy, do their pronouncements matter to the folks in white at the stoves.

Should you ever find yourself in the position of sitting in the editor's chair overseeing one of these food bibles here's a tip – a good first move is to book your holiday to coincide with publication date. Actually, that's probably not foolproof either – they'll find you. During my tenure, I had calls to my home number, my wife's restaurant and one guy even turned up to harangue me in the local pub. Nobody, as far as I know, actually threatened to take their life or mine, but there is no shortage of affronted chefs queuing up to tell you that you've 'ruined their life', 'destroyed their career' or cost them several thousand pounds in bonus payments.

So why do some of those at the stove take it so seriously? Well, yes, there is the issue of career advancement – an additional star or rosette can add thousands to salary expectations, and there is probably *some* impact on business levels, although as I've argued, that's probably minimal. Most of all it's about status and recognition. The guidebooks offer the most tangible reward in this respect and are the accepted indicator of a chef's standing among his peers. Almost anyone cooking half-decent food has a rating of some sort which means they can be conveniently labelled and ranked on the ladder of culinary achievement.

And pretty much everyone buys into the process to one degree or another, which is kind of remarkable because the great unspoken truth is that the practice of inspecting restaurants for food guides is about as accurate and reliable as compiling the accounts of a multinational corporation. Just look at the logistics. There are maybe 40,000 restaurants in the UK and even the biggest inspection teams number fewer than thirty people. That means only a small proportion of the total number is ever visited by any guide and those will mostly be the same ones in each book because all the guides feed off each other's information. Then consider that most of these restaurants will get only one visit in a twelve-month period, which makes the inspection nothing more than a snapshot – things occasionally go wrong in every kitchen. And then there's the whole question of the criteria for a rating. Yes, we can try and assess the quality of the produce, the accuracy of the cooking, the intelligence of the flavour combinations, but in the end it is a constant struggle to make a subjective assessment as objective as possible and to get a group of very different individual inspectors to look for exactly the same things in wildly different styles of food.

Not an easy process then, and truthfully it's one that will never be much more than a general indicator of where's good and where's bad to eat. Logic suggests then that no one should take the outcome too seriously. But the reality is that the chefs *do*, and that means there is for the guides a weight of responsibility that they have to accept. In the judgements they make there will always be worries about accuracy, thoroughness and those marginal decisions that could arguably go one way or the other, but at the very least they must be honest. Honest about the frailty of the inspection system, honest in trying to make the best of an imperfect job and above all honest in their decision-making. The inspection system might be deeply flawed but in principle the major independent guides at least claim to make it a level playing field without favour or prejudice. When even that basic tenet is challenged – as I felt it was over the AA's treatment of London's Petrus restaurant in the run-up to the 2003 guide – then you've failed in that obligation, and the chefs deserve better than that.

Marcus Wareing, the head chef at Petrus, was not somebody I knew, but I was aware of the typically long hours that he puts in as he strives for success. In 2002, with the 2003 edition of the guide being prepared for publication, he was in line for the AA's highest award, five rosettes. A number of inspectors had been and made a positive recommendation; then the chief inspector made a last visit, and he too recommended five rosettes. Petrus had been in line for the award the previous year too. I had made the final visit myself then, and it was my call. After a bit of deliberation I decided it was close but not quite there yet, but it was named Restaurant of the Year in any case. This time around there was no doubt. Petrus deserved five rosettes and it would get them – after a fashion.

Roger Wood had been appointed managing director at the AA from his previous post at British Gas, part of the parent company, Centrica, who had bought the AA a few years before (and have now decided it wasn't such a bright idea after all and disposed of it again). This man was running the whole AA show, the principal business being the rescue service but with a significant financial services division too. Publishing is a small part of the AA picture, and the biggest share of that is the maps. The *AA Restaurant Guide* is just a tiny dot on the landscape of the AA, way down in some quiet valley of the organisation and barely visible to the man at the top. There was talk of cost-cutting – there always is – but we felt fairly safe. Not really fat and juicy enough to attract the attention of the birds of prey preening themselves at the top of the mountain. And anyway, Roger already looked pretty well fed to me.

Roger Wood went to Petrus. Not to eat, but to check on a reservation he'd made for an important engagement with some business colleagues. It was his intention to select a particular table but the restaurant manager was unable to guarantee a specific location that far in advance. Roger decided that this was a good time to let them know who he was. Managing director of the AA, who publish the *AA Restaurant Guide* and who made Petrus Restaurant of the Year. None of this changed the situation with the table because that depended on the bookings that came in between then and the date of the meal. Roger was not amused. He fired off emails, he summoned the managers in publishing to meetings, he made it clear that Petrus would not receive five rosettes in the 2003 guide.

Now this kind of thing happens in big companies and in my experience there tends to be a lot of huff and puff before the whole thing blows over and sanity is restored. I made it clear that if the final decision on Petrus was going to be made in this way, disregarding the recommendation of the inspectors and being determined by the whim of the MD, then I'd have to resign, but I honestly didn't expect it to come to that. Three months later, when the book was about to go to print, I found myself doing just that. Roger was apparently adamant that Petrus would not receive five rosettes.

Although I'd had three months to think about it, the final outcome still shook me. I was out of a job, with nothing immediate to go to. I told the whole story to the *Caterer and Hotelkeeper* magazine who ran it over half a dozen pages. The national newspapers picked it up and it ran as a big story in all of them (with the exception of the *Sun*). The AA started backtracking and within days announced that the decision would be reviewed. Before the week was out, they had awarded Petrus five rosettes after all.

Why did it take my resignation and all the resulting bad PR for the AA to arrive at the only legitimate decision? I can't be sure, but one thing I do know is that some at the AA weren't taking the awards seriously enough, they weren't discharging their responsibility to the chefs they assessed. The sort of phrases that were repeated to me were 'Why make a fuss, Simon? What does it matter? Marcus Wareing won't know any different, it'll have been forgotten by next year, he can have his five rosettes then.' It was a frivolous attitude and I think maybe some of that is explained by a lack of understanding of the realities of life in a restaurant kitchen and in particular by ignorance of what it takes to get that near to the top of the tree.

That's partly what drove me to write this book – to fill at least some of that gap in the perception of the effort needed to make the upper reaches of the culinary profession. I also wrote it because I've met a lot of young chefs who tell me that one day they're going to be another Gordon Ramsay or whoever – well, maybe they'll read this and appreciate that it won't happen by accident.

And finally I wrote it because, although I spent a good deal of time on the other side of the fence, I've always had a high regard for those who weather the harsh climate of the kitchen. I once saw Anthony Bourdain of *Kitchen Confidential* fame give a talk in which he spoke about the 'brotherhood' of chefs, the right to a certain swagger that you get only from having proved yourself at the heat of the stove. The chapters that follow tell the very distinct tales of four chefs who have risen through that brotherhood to make a special mark on their profession.

Theirs is an elite band, tough to join, and these are the stories of how they qualified for membership.

GORDON RAMSAY

Way Beyond Boiling Point

Lunch is coming to an end and Gordon Ramsay's Michelin-starred restaurant is now almost empty. Besides a couple of American ladies in unyielding hairdos finishing their decaf, and a suspicious lone diner, it's just me and the chef. I'm seated, but opposite me Gordon Ramsay is on his feet, bent double and clutching his buttocks. 'Right in the f***ing crack,' he says, pulling the cheeks apart to emphasise the point. I look around nervously; it appears we're obscured from the remaining diners. This comes as a relief – I'm a big fan of his cooking and I can't deny that it's satisfying to walk through the tables in his company – but I'm not sure I'm ready for anyone to see him splaying his backside for my benefit.

It's a generous act though, and he can be a generous man. He has a lot on his plate – this restaurant at Claridges, Restaurant Gordon Ramsay in Chelsea, Angela Hartnett at the Connaught, an interest in Restaurant Petrus in St James which is about to move to the Berkeley

Hotel, the opening of the Boxwood Café also at the Berkeley Hotel, input into his protégé Marcus Wareing's takeover of the Savoy Grill, the new restaurant Maze in Grosvenor Square and forthcoming projects in Tokyo and New York – but he's still willing to spend energy reliving his past for my benefit. Actually it doesn't appear to be much of an effort. He talks fast and with passion. It's as if the extraordinary journey of the past twenty years is flitting in front of his eyes, episode by episode, and all he can do is frantically relay what he sees, almost in disbelief. It's high drama all the way from evoking the 'shitfight' of Marco Pierre White's revolutionary kitchen at Harvey's – 'if they'd filmed it, it would be an Oscar nominee' – to acting out Albert Roux's perfectly directed kick in the rear (see above) for a transgression in the kitchens of Le Gavroche. When I leave, I'm exhilarated and thankful. Thankful for the chance to have heard the tale firsthand, thankful that he agreed to give me his time and strangely grateful, for the first time since it happened, that I lost my job because of one of his restaurants.

Because, let's be honest, without that incident, how else would I have ended up sitting in one of the world's most celebrated hotels, watching one of the world's greatest chefs enthusiastically grabbing at his own behind.

Maybe I'm being over generous, but British hotel food is by and large repellent. For years my vocation was to stay in hotels, eat, and report back on whether they were up to standard or not. Generally they were, but that is only because the bar was set so pitifully low. When I hear people whining on radio talk shows about British prisons being like hotels, my mind drifts back to dismal nights in cramped conditions with the company of chipped white melamine, a decade of dust and tannin-stained teacups. If prisons are like that, I'm staying straight. As an aid to lowering the spirits, *nothing* is as effective as entering a bog standard two- or three-star hotel room, contemplating the cheerless scenery and realising you are going to be alone there until eight o'clock the next morning. *Nothing*, that is, other than going down to the restaurant and taking a look at the menu.

For a lot of hotels the restaurant is little more than an encumbrance. The money is in the rooms, where all you have to do is change the beds, swill out the cups in the washbasin and if pressed, change the batteries in the remote control. Restaurants require chefs, waiting staff and perishable stock. The margins are low and it's a lot of effort for not much return, if any. Many hotels would happily dispense with their restaurants if it wasn't for the requirements of their star ratings. Maybe the tourist boards should declare an amnesty – give up your restaurants and we'll turn a blind eye. You can keep your stars. Millions would rejoice.

But then we'd lose the breeding ground for the kitchen talent of the future, like the three-star hotel on the outskirts of Stratford-upon-Avon where Gordon Ramsay first entered a commercial kitchen. It was instructional, but not in terms of how to cook. 'What did kick in was how wrong things were … it was shocking, I mean shockingly bad, mange tout and green beans tossed in butter, put in the hotplate and left, roast potatoes that had been dipped and blanched in the fryer, drained, then seasoned with Bovril ... the granulated Bovril, all over it in the roasting tray ... Beef cooked off at eight-thirty or nine o'clock in the morning and then left ...'

Gordon's mother worked in a tearoom called the Cobweb in Stratford-upon-Avon. 'I'd go to meet her after work in this hot sweaty kitchen and there was a pastry chef called Roland, an immense, six foot six, strapping pastry chef and I was just obsessed with the way he was so focused on making éclairs.' Together with the stuff she brought home from work – glazed hams, homemade curries, stews and soups – it was enough to make him realise, when he entered that first hotel kitchen, that something was badly awry. 'I just knew my mum could do better. I just knew that, God, *a* this was a very famous restaurant to work in and *b* it was run by Italians in the dining room.' As a consequence, he'd expected something better – passion, craft, dedication. What he got was an idle lump of a chef who was working hard at an easy life, 'a big, huge, fat, bald-headed guy, who was just in a foul temper, and all he wanted to do was get the work done as quick as possible, so we just ploughed through things and what I realised early was there was just no *care*.' His face screws up in a mixture of sadness and disbelief at the thought of it. 'No *attention*.'

Indolence is clearly not big with him. When he talks about his reasons for entering catering in the first place it's a common story of accident over design (the sad truth, as a director of a catering college once told me, is that for most catering students their presence is a

4

matter of geography – if they're not there, they're on the streets) but also of a nagging work ethic. 'Really there were two choices: to go into a day release as a commis or to go into the police force.' The police force was ruled out because of a lack of qualifications – 'I got two O levels' – and so he was steered towards cooking 'because it was not right to stand in limbo with nothing to do'.

Given his age and recent history he might have been forgiven a period of self-indulgent moping around. Spotted as a schoolboy talent at Oxford United he had been whisked off to Glasgow to join Rangers in a squad that also included promising youngsters such as Ally McCoist, Derek Ferguson and Dave McPherson. Unlike them, he was eventually let go. It has to be quite a blow in your late teens, to have been sucked into that heady environment with the promise of a career in top-flight football, and then just as quickly let down. Personally, I'd have sulked for a decade, at least.

But Gordon Ramsay looked for something else to throw himself into. Things weren't great at home with a heavy-drinking father whose habit had led to the break-up of the marriage. Although working at the hotel was grim and uninspiring, he was saved by his day a week at catering college. 'College was the release, but that was my day off because we used to work six days a week and of course the bastards at the hotel made me do f***ing breakfast in the morning before I went to college. I fell out with Dad ... and we hadn't spoken. Him and Mum were going through a bad divorce at the time and I just ploughed myself into it.' Some of the staff at the college were also helping to fill a gap, and served as inspiration. Norma John, an 'amazing' pastry chef who made wonderful wedding cakes (years later she made him a gift of the cake when he married Tana) and Alistair Hawthorn, a Savoy-trained chef and later a food and beverage manager who had 'gone through the mill, a strong, thorough Scottish man [who] reminded me of Dad ...' There's a pause, '... when he was nice. You respected him so much because he was so correct.'

The requirements of catering college demanded that Ramsay put in time front of house as well as in the kitchen. This at least meant he was able to eliminate waiting as a possible career path. 'In the dining room I was just useless, too clumsy. I remember there was the waiter, Miguel, he'd turn around and say "You're like horseshit, you're always in the middle of the road, get out of the f***ing way."' For the most part though, he was learning to cook, but this was shortcut cuisine with the emphasis on speed, profit margins and quantity. Quality was an afterthought. He was working hard and was well thought of at college but spent the majority of his time turning out the likes of veal cordon bleu, deep-fried whitebait from frozen, tournedos Rossini with tinned pâté – classic British hotel cooking and hardly the stuff that legendary chefs are nourished on.

☆☆☆

Caterer and Hotelkeeper, packed as it is with job adverts, is ever present in the staff rooms of UK hotels. London's Mayfair Intercontinental was opening a new banqueting suite, the Crystal Room, and it featured on the front cover. The Mayfair wasn't up there with the Savoy or the Dorchester but it was a big luxury hotel in the capital, it looked glitzy and exciting, and Ramsay remembers being impressed by the 'marvellous logo'. He applied for a job, went for an interview and found himself working in a good London kitchen – in banqueting. 'That was amazing, because it was London for the first time, there was a bedsit with my mate who got a job at the Royal Garden ... I was working under Billy King and then Michael Coker.' These were big names in the industry, but grand London hotel kitchens are massive operations with legions of chefs and people joining and leaving on a daily basis. For a second commis chef grade 2 those at the top of the pile were distant figures and, although there was a buzz to working at an important hotel in the capital, in the kitchen he was churning out function food and his growing thirst for knowledge wasn't really being sated. 'It was weird because I spent a year there and it was happening, but it wasn't. The banquets were 200 covers, [whereas] the Chateau [the fine-dining restaurant] was something special and they left the French chefs to do that.'

The bedsit was expensive, at least in relation to his basic wages, but fortunately the Mayfair, somewhat unusually, paid overtime. Ramsay grabbed all he could get. One night, when he'd already worked a triple shift of breakfast, lunch and dinner, the night chef didn't turn up and he stayed on. 'I'll never forget it ever. I worked through-out the night ... At four o'clock in the morning I was completely f***ed, shattered. I'd done all my mise en place [getting certain

7

items ready prior to service], boxed all that off and I went back to the staff canteen to take a drink.' A copy of *Caterer and Hotelkeeper* had been left lying around, on the cover a picture of Marco Pierre White. 'His first interview, two weeks after he opened Harvey's and I read it and I listened to the upset, how he lost his mum, how he didn't get on with his father, what the guy was about. He was six years older than me, he was in the kitchen and he had a blue apron on, which only the hotel butcher wore, he didn't wear a necktie, he didn't wear a hat, he had a pair of trainers on. So I thought *Jesus*.' He was captivated. For the second time in quick succession a magazine cover had sparked a defining change of direction. As a method of making career choices, it has served him well enough, but it does make you grateful that nobody had left a copy of *True Crimes* hanging around – by now he'd be doing life.

Of course, it isn't as simple as reading a story and thinking you quite fancy some of that; there's the small matter of doing something about it. And it's always easier not to, that way you avoid disappointment. I don't do the lottery, that way I'm guaranteed not to lose. Oddly enough I haven't won either.

'So Saturday morning I phoned him and he was in there – the restaurant was closed but he was there, opening his mail ... I lied about my experience and he told me to come over, there and then. I didn't expect him to answer the telephone ... *Jesus Christ*, you know, "Who is this?" and he was like blunt beyond blunt. But that was it and that's when it *really* started, that was the turnaround and I've never forgotten that and I'll never deny it.'

London in 2005 is a city fat with good places to eat. A city that can pat its satisfied belly, wave its napkin at the world and belch a demand for culinary comparison with the likes of Paris, Milan and Madrid, without fear of laughter. A hungry man on a pavement of the capital can hail a taxi, bark an instruction to 'Follow that aroma' and find himself heading to almost any quarter. North to Clerkenwell, to tear a rare pig from 'nose to tail' with Fergus Henderson at St John or to enjoy tapas, sweet Serrano ham and dressed broad beans at nearby Moro. To Mayfair, where the cumbersome theatre of grand hotel dining rooms has been overthrown in favour of dexterity, freshness and lightness of touch by the likes of Gordon Ramsay and Marcus Wareing. South of the river to the earthy comfort of Waterloo's Anchor and Hope; a chick to Farringdon's Eagle – places ill-served by the ugly tag of 'gastropub'. Out west to Chiswick for the simple French bistro cooking of La Trompette, or even further into the setting sun, down the M4 to Bray and Heston Blumenthal's amused trickery at the Fat Duck.

A couple of decades ago, to suggest that such riches might one day descend upon us would have seemed risible. Not even a daydreaming over-optimist at the London Tourist Board, idly staring out of a rose-tinted window, would have thought to toy with the idea that this city might become known for the quality and range of its restaurants. It was an outcome that then seemed as unlikely as an English-born chef becoming the youngest ever recipient of the fabled three Michelin stars, a Labour government securing successive landslide election victories or Wales winning the Rugby World Cup (it *will* happen, believe me). Twenty years ago you either mortgaged your house for a perfect morsel of French fine dining at the likes of Le Gavroche or the Waterside, or you pretty much had to put up with fraudulent and weary versions of European classics such as tournedos Rossini, chicken cacciatore or coq au vin. What we have now was just not imaginable then, not on the agenda, not part of anyone's manifesto ... and yet it has come to pass, without a White Paper on improving British restaurants, without a party policy loftily promising to bring us up to European standards of cuisine, without a grant-aided campaign to pump-prime an explosion in decent dining. Nobody sat and planned this revolution by cabal or committee and yet in the late 1980s a series of insurgencies sprang up across the capital and what had been the slow stirrings of change suddenly stiffened into a full-force gale. The culinary landscape of London would be changed for ever by the rapid emergence of restaurants such as Bibendum in Fulham Road, River Café in Hammersmith, Kensington Place in, well, Kensington Place, Alistair Little in Frith Street and Harvey's in Bellevue Road, SW17.

Nothing would be quite the same again on the British restaurant scene. This was a defining moment in British cooking that set Marco Pierre White and Gordon Ramsay on the path that would lead them both, in turn, to become the new king of British cooking. Among the public, other chefs may be better known, but in terms of impact on British eating out, their achievements in the kitchen and their status among their fellow chefs, they have dominated the last fifteen years. This happened because a night chef missed his shift, because a copy of *Caterer and Hotelkeeper* was left lying around in a staff canteen, because White happened to be in the restaurant on the day that it was shut, because it was he who answered the phone rather than somebody else, and because he happened to be looking for another pair of hands. It could happen to anyone. Anyone who bothered to make that telephone call.

Ramsay couldn't have known exactly what he was walking into, but he had clearly sensed that there was something uncommon happening at Harvey's, that its charismatic young chef with the wild tentacles of dark hair, whose background was similar to his own, was embarking on something radical. He was drawn there by the electricity which would surge through him – fizzing, crackling and occasionally igniting – for the next two years and ten months. He went in as a kitchen hand and emerged as a chef.

☆☆☆

Chefs are artists, aren't they? We see them on television tossing ingredients into a pan almost intuitively, cooking on the hoof, looking inspired, lost in the act of creating. Some of them have crazy hairstyles, some have tantrums, one even wears a bandanna, so he *must* be an artist. Flair, natural talent, creativity – that's what a kitchen wants from a chef, isn't it? So if you're considering a profession in which you can express yourself, break boundaries, do things differently ... Consider looking elsewhere.

The skill that is most cherished in formal fine-dining kitchens is the willingness to obey orders. It's no coincidence that kitchen brigades are organised on the same hierarchical lines as an army. The leaders demand personal discipline and when that slips, discipline is enforced from above. A chef's first responsibility is to learn a task and keep repeating it in exactly the same way, to precisely the same standard. It's about doing the same thing, over and over and over again. That's how these restaurants achieve the consistency that keeps both the customers and the Michelin inspectors happy. These chefs are artists all right, but 99 per cent are in the same position as the artists that carried out the donkey work for the likes of Leonardo – drawing to instruction, painting by numbers. It's skilled work that requires dedication and persistence, and then perhaps one day, just maybe, after a decade or so of sweat, you get to play the Leonardo role. But until then, it's not about being different, it's about being the same.

Such kitchens dominate the higher reaches of British cooking. Marco Pierre White had been in the best of them, seen how it was done and learnt the rules. Crucially though, he not only knew the rules but understood why they were there and had come to comprehend the principles that underpinned them. He was then in his early thirties and in charge of his own restaurant, so why shouldn't he make his own laws – whether that related to kitchen dress or breaking culinary convention? He had a hungry talent, immense self-belief, a clear vision and a small, tight team that believed in him. He was 'a man on a mission' as Gordon Ramsay puts it. A fly-on-the-wall documentary of Harvey's would have made a guaranteed Hollywood blockbuster, reckons Ramsay, but there was no secret camera filming these scenes, only the lens of Bob Carlos Clarke, whose iconographic black and white photographs would illustrate *White Heat*, Marco Pierre White's first book of recipes. In it there are pictures of the dishes, but it's the portraits in the kitchen that make you pause: Marco working intensely at the stove, Marco lighting up, Marco fooling around with the rest of the kitchen team. The unkempt dark hair dominates the close-ups, together with the penetrating gaze and dark bags under the eyes that speak of relentless drive and dedication. He looks youthful, determined and utterly knackered, but more than anything he looks like a young man who is supremely confident of his destiny. Examine the photographs, read the self-penned text and you'll be left in little doubt. Harvey's was a Marco Pierre White-led rebellion and *White Heat* was the manifesto.

There was no more zealous recruit to the cause than Gordon Ramsay. This was his new home, a second family, entered into with a clean sheet. 'Marco knew nothing about the football because that was a cardinal rule, no one knew anything about that, *nothing*. I didn't want them to start making leeway, doing me any special favours and, of course, I had the cut off from Dad so I had no baggage ... I walked into that kitchen, I thought *my God*. We've gone from twenty-five to thirty cooks in a kitchen to like four ... This guy was boning out pigeons, he was chopping shallots, picking spinach, he was making tagliatelle and it was like *Jesus* this is me, I've found my base. I've found me. I wanted it.'

And he must have wanted it very badly. Easier lives were available to him. In fact, almost anything would have been easier. It's doubtful that any kitchen has delivered quite that level of harshness, demanded such reserves of stamina and provided such challenging conditions in which to work. The intensity was unparalleled and for Gordon Ramsay it came to represent a rite of passage into serious cooking, if he could take this he could take whatever was thrown at him, and he would never face anything quite as tough again in his career. 'The flak was amazing. I've never ever gone through a period of taking so much flak in my life … it was raw, but brilliantly raw and raw that you actually enjoyed it, in the sense that when you really f***ed up and you made a big mistake you *wanted* to take a bollocking, big time, because the better the bollocking the stronger you became.'

Harvey's fed him. With every battering his skin thickened. He was learning what could be achieved by sheer determination and single-mindedness, learning that there is little time for niceties in the frenzy of a service, learning how to cook at the highest level, but most of all he was learning how to taste.

No big deal there, surely. We all know how to taste: just open your mouth, insert an object and let your tongue do the work – simple. In fact, for the young chef it was a priceless gift, the ability to review his own work, examine it, criticise it and refine it. To taste one element – a stock or a wine reduction, say – and know just when it is right for its intended purpose in a sauce; to check seasoning, the balance of flavours in a dish and fine tune them. Without this skill a chef at the stove is like a musician working without sound: you can play the notes as instructed but you can't trim, adjust and finesse the music based on what you're hearing – you're trusting to luck, and the results are likely to be mixed at best. In a chef's repertoire, tasting is a fundamental tool. You wouldn't catch a painter working blindfold, would you? No. Would you find a chef who didn't taste? Well, strange as it may seem, it's like looking for dry grass in a haystack.

Have you ever had a meal that was unbelievably salty or tongue-numbingly bland? Well, it's unlikely that the chef actually intended it to be that way. It's almost certainly attributable to the fact that he or she simply doesn't taste. A little while ago a junior chef asked me what I thought of the consistency of his risotto. When I said I thought it was perfect, he was reassured. 'But how about the seasoning, how about the taste?' he asked anxiously. 'Maybe a little restrained,' I said. 'What do you think?' He looked at me blankly. 'Well, I dunno, I don't really eat that sort of thing.' In one form or another, I've heard that a hundred times.

When Gordon Ramsay is dishing out the tributes to what he learned under White (and he does this fulsomely and with no hint of rivalry) it's this that takes priority. 'The guy was awesome and vibrant and wild and *he taught me how to taste*. He drummed it into me.' The work was varied and each day delivered bright nuggets of information that were eagerly seized and banked in a store of culinary knowledge that was increasing at an exponential rate.

'... just the way everything was cooked to order. I'd never been in an establishment where we made soups to order. Like the potage of shellfish. It was one ladle of nage, one ladle of oyster juice and one ladle of velouté. Bring that up to the boil, scallops in, oyster in, chervil in, tagliatelle of cucumber, finish with a little caviar and serve.'

With just four in the kitchen, maybe fifteen to twenty customers for lunch and a further sixty covers in the evening, this kind of labour-intensive cooking inevitably meant two things – little rest and not much play. 'It was manic, we were in the kitchen at seven to seven fifteen and we weren't out before one o'clock [the next morning]. And then the bombshell was when Marco was looking to expand and he turned around with his then business partner Nigel Platts Martin and said, "We're going to be open Saturday lunchtime now." So, of course, all the chefs out in the countryside came to eat on Saturday lunch so Saturday was one headf*** day. And we used to lie on the common for a sort of fifteen to twenty-minute break and he was adamant we wouldn't play football any more because we used to get too dirty … so we just used to lie on our backs and peel the *girolles*, lying there looking at these aeroplanes.' Sundays would mean sleeping in until maybe six in the evening, getting up and launching themselves on the town, having dinner and then partying at the Rock Garden until 1 a.m. Instead of returning home they'd head for Wandsworth and the restaurant. There they'd sleep on the banquettes just to make sure they were on time the following morning.

Whichever dimension you look at, it was a frighteningly tight situation. There was no slack in terms of either time or physical space. Once the gun went off it was a frantic effort to keep all the plates spinning, powering through the occasional crash and speeding headlong towards the end of service, only to begin it all again. 'You'd get to twelve thirty at lunchtime and the first order would come on. Tagliatelle of oysters, which was the most amazing dish, beautiful tagliatelle, poached oysters, velouté, caviar. And we'd have no tag there because he wanted it done to order. The pasta's made but it's not rolled and he'd say, "We roll it if we need it," but there were like ten other things to do at the same time. And ... because there was no such thing as a pass there − it was a table − and where my chopping board was we had a stick ... and all the tickets were on there so I had to work over them ... boning out this and boning out that. And I made some hellish mistakes. But I tell you, he taught me the basics and it was a fundamental insight into brilliance.'

That recognition of his special gift meant that White could demand, and largely got, an almost unquestioning loyalty. Allegiance was to him alone and there was no room for even the temptation of infidelity. He dismissed a junior cook who was sharing Ramsay's flat. Although Ramsay disagreed with the sacking, that in itself wouldn't have been enough to rupture the relationship. But White pushed it much further: 'Marco then wanted me to go back after service that night and throw him out in the street, because if he was still living in my flat and if I came to work for Marco, [he felt] this guy was still part of his kitchen ... [It was] psychological torment and I just said to Marco ... "Love you to death, love my job, the most fascinating job I've ever had in my life but I can't do that." He said, "Then you're *sacked*. You leave in two weeks' time." He made me sit there and listen to him while he phoned John Burton Race at L'Ortolan to send two cooks down to replace me. I walked back down to the kitchen, I was upset, I was crying, my eyes were full of water, my little brother Ronnie was in the plonge, it was about a quarter past six, Marco never came down before seven o'clock and I just walked out ... five minutes later I'd taken my whites off ... The train station was opposite the back door and I jumped on a train and went back [to the flat]. We (Ramsay and his flatmate chef) had a shower, got changed and went out. And we got *absolutely* smashed. Woke up Saturday morning and what Marco had actually done was call the customers to say there'd been a gas leak so he could close the restaurant that night, because I cooked fish and meat, there was no one else there who could do it ... On the Sunday he tracked me down, I took his call and he said, "This is stupid, we've got to talk." So I walked back, I had everything booked for a two-week holiday, but I cancelled it all and started back on the Monday. I thought Christ I'm giving everything I've got ... my entire life.'

☆☆☆

It was a claustrophobic, isolated life, largely lived in the confines of the kitchen box. Fatigue became a constant companion, a permanent shadow to be coped with but rarely shaken off. The chefs took in a sugary diet of Twix and Lucozade, standing one foot atop the other, knees locked, as they peeled and scraped, drifting into periods of semi-consciousness – trying to snatch whatever minutes of rest they could before service came on. But, of course, when battle commenced, the adrenalin kicked in and the tiredness fell away. Ramsay was part of a crusade that, despite the choking hours, awkward working conditions, relentless demand for quality and frequent dressing downs, compelled him to stay. Although his experience of top-level cooking was limited, it was obvious to him that he was part of something special, and White knew the importance of driving the team on, fuelling their motivation and keeping the desire going. 'It was a journey and we were cut off. The only time we were able to realise how important it was, was when you went out to eat. He sent us all to the Waterside (Michel Roux's three-star restaurant) and that helped to confirm where Harvey's was and that's not being detrimental to the Waterside, but it showed me how brilliant Harvey's was. He was insistent [on his team eating out], he sent us to Le Gavroche … It was a very clever way of showing us how good we were becoming because of what he'd taught us and he got more back then.'

And White wanted a lot back. Although he had a loyal team around him, he was the one with the experience, the complete set of skills, it was his vision and his name above the door. In the kitchen he gave them limited leeway. He worked on a system of intense scrutiny with tight control. If they filleted a turbot, the bones had to be left so they could be examined to see how clean they were; only Marco could finish the sauces in case they put too much veal jus in. Trust was too risky a strategy. One mistake could blow everything – including the chef's cool. One night an order came in for a vegetarian customer

– leek terrine. A simple enough request, but the terrine was actually leek and shellfish with the seafood left out of one end of the block so that it could be sliced independently and served as vegetarian. White asked which end he should be slicing. Ramsay told him left, and that there was a blue plaster on one end to flag up the leek-only section. Maybe he didn't see the plaster, maybe the terrine got turned around, maybe Ramsay's left was White's right. Whatever the reason, there was lobster in it. 'He said, "You're f***ing lying!" and I said, "No, no, it's the other end!" But of course he wouldn't even attempt to do it because he thought I'd forgotten ... and he picked up the whole terrine and just threw the whole thing at me.' Ramsay, ostensibly, headed off to get some oysters, but with escape on his mind, he got past White and bolted. White took off in pursuit. In the bar a couple of newly arrived customers watched as the chefs screamed past, out of the door and into the street, full pelt down the road. White was faster – 'over a hundred yards he would have had me' – but Ramsay had enough of a start to stay clear. It was his second and last unplanned exit – he would quickly return to the fold – but after two years, his confidence was growing and he had begun to think of the future. In his mind he started to contemplate a horizon beyond the strict confines of Harvey's, beyond London and beyond the British Isles.

☆☆☆

Think of great cooking and you must think of France. I insist. Yes, there are caveats — the relative rise in cooking standards in other countries, an arrogance and complacency in French cooking (that has in some instances resulted in a stubborn refusal to adapt, innovate or develop), and the over-theatrical service of sometimes mediocre food — but notwithstanding all that, it remains the beating heart of cuisine. The classic dishes, the techniques and the structure of kitchens are all derived from across the Channel. The great London chefs of that time had either migrated from there or were directly descended from great French kitchens. It was, and is, the culinary Mecca and Ramsay could feel himself being called to prayer. With the help of the French restaurant manager at Harvey's, Ramsay organised a season with the great French chef Alain Ducasse at La Terrasse in Juan-les-Pins. It was a good plan and a great break for a young chef but there was a fatal flaw. White wasn't going to let go of the reins that easily. 'Marco went mad and he got [the restaurant manager] and f***ed him for trying to get me the job.' Ramsay was told to stay and a place would be arranged for him at Le Gavroche [Albert Roux's restaurant is as close to France as you can get while remaining in London], then he could go with Marco's good wishes, but not just yet. According to White, Le Gavroche was full and he'd have to wait another year. In retrospect Ramsay believes he paid the price for stepping out of line and taking the initiative without seeking the approval of his mentor. 'I know, deep down inside that if I'd asked Marco to get me a job, without any bullshit, I'd have been there within a month because Michel [Roux Jnr of Le Gavroche] would have taken me. But Marco said, "No, the kitchen's full, do another ten months, we'll move you in there, go with my blessing, you'll get looked after." Looked after! I got panned. They didn't want to see *any* of Marco there.'

Such are the benefits of patronage. Ramsay was about to start again, almost on the bottom rung, but he was no longer the fresh-faced innocent who had walked through the doors of Harvey's nearly three years before. He had worked with a remarkable, uniquely talented chef in the white heat that had forged a legendary restaurant – achieving two Michelin stars in three years. He had seen genius in the kitchen at first hand, witnessed an uncompromising struggle for perfection and he had come to understand the relationship between brilliance and hard slog. Marco Pierre White really needn't have worried about giving him his blessing – he'd already blessed him plentifully.

☆ ☆ ☆

If Marco Pierre White had made the journey from the highly disciplined environment of the top formal kitchens to the freewheeling, seat of the pants job that was Harvey's, Gordon Ramsay was about to do the reverse. It was as if Ringo had left the Beatles for the Royal Philharmonic Orchestra – playing the triangle. Ramsay was back to being a simple commis chef, one up from the kitchen porter. From earning a substantial £750 a month now he was receiving £528 and was obliged to wear a hat and an apron. If Marco had been watchful and prescriptive about what his chefs produced, that was nothing compared to the rigours of Le Gavroche, where there was zero flexibility in producing the dishes. But there were upsides too – on-the-go meals of chocolate bars and energy drinks were replaced by the unfamiliar practice of sitting down to eat lunch and dinner. There was also the extraordinary privilege of weekends off, although Ramsay, finding it hard to let go of the buzz provided by Harvey's, wasn't taking full advantage of that particular benefit. He had reached the point where he had White's full trust and for the first six months at Le Gavroche he worked Saturday nights at Harvey's in order that White could have a proper evening off. 'I used to get paid £50 quid … he felt if I was in that kitchen there'd never be any problem so he could take a proper night off.'

With the maximum three Michelin stars, Le Gavroche was at that time a legend of British restaurants. Established by the French brothers Michel and Albert Roux in 1967 it was classic, grand French dining brought to the UK. The brothers had come to Britain to work in the kitchens of rich patrons and between them they went on to establish both Le Gavroche and then the Waterside Inn at Bray in Berkshire. These restaurants in turn became the nursery for much of the cooking talent that has emerged in the UK since. Marco Pierre White was one example, Gordon Ramsay was to be another and Marcus Wareing, Michael Caines, Gary Rhodes all served apprenticeships in them.

And apprenticeship is the right word. Nothing was left to chance at Le Gavroche, nothing happened on the whim of junior chefs. To

Ramsay the organisation and thoroughness of the approach to cooking was a revelation. A tailor-made recipe set determined the preparation of each dish down to the smallest detail, and there was zero flexibility in its execution, not a thing left to chance. This was not the place to suggest changes, contribute menu ideas, look to impose a little of his own style or even hint at the quality of dishes from Harvey's. 'You mention a tagliatelle of oysters, stuffed seabass with a caviar sauce … kiss your bum goodbye.'

Almost literally in Ramsay's case.

Although he had handed over the kitchen to his son Michel, Albert Roux was still often to be found on the pass, that sacred strip of stainless steel where the dishes receive a final examination prior to leaving the kitchen. He may have taken a step back and allowed himself luxuries such as a glass of champagne at his side, but his ability to detect even a faint stutter in the purring engine of the kitchen remained undiminished. Shrewd and owlish, he cast an impassive eye over proceedings, tuned into the rattle of pans and the choreography of the chefs in their crisp whites, ready to swoop upon the smallest discrepancy. Young chefs who thought they could get away with the odd shortcut or could pull the wool over the older man's eyes were destined to be swiftly caught out.

On the hot starters, with a dozen things on the go and afflicted with the nervousness that goes hand-in-hand with the fragile art of cooking a soufflé, Ramsay was tempted to take a peek at its progress. This was a forbidden act as it opened the possibility of collapse and instead, typically, the practice was for the chef to count out the timing in his head and not open the door till the exact period had elapsed. Ramsay, unable to resist, pulled the door ajar, just a little, and took a quick look at the soufflé, which was perfect. As he turned away he let go of the heavy oven door which delivered a telltale clunk as it sprung back. The noise didn't go unnoticed by Albert, but he chose the timing of his reprimand with care. '... he knew that I'd opened the door. But he just waited two or three minutes and when I came past him he gave me the biggest boot up my arse and it went *right* inside the crack and it f***ing hurt ... and then he turned around and said, "I told you not to touch the door," so it was just amazing how he had that all planned and he set my arse up and he took a swing at it ... and I admired him for that because he'd just done it properly and he'd waited until he was in perfect position and he'd let me know not to touch that oven door because I should be counting in my head.'

As an ex-footballer, Ramsay could be expected to appreciate the beauty of a well-timed boot, but it was Roux's rigour and ability to detect bullshit that most impressed him. To achieve the fingertip precision of the cooking at Le Gavroche he needed to be sure that everything was being carried out precisely as dictated and he therefore needed the chefs to know that they could get away with nothing. And in establishing that climate in the kitchen, his verbal technique could be just as impressive as his martial arts.

Friday lunch could be sixty to seventy covers all à la carte without the cushion of a more limited lunch menu. On a typically hectic service the older Roux was again running the pass and Ramsay faced a relentless fight to keep up with the pace of orders. The master took the opportunity to teach the pupil a lesson. Ramsay, struggling to keep all the balls in the air, faced a series of rapid-fire questions from Albert.

'He said, "Have you got the saumon Claudine?"'

'I said, "Yes, chef."'

'"Have you got the mousseline d'homard?"'

'I said, "Oui, chef."'

'"Have you got the baked lobster?"'

'I said, "Oui."'

'He said, "How many?"'

'I said, "Two."'

'He said, "You're a f***ing lying bastard because there's none on order!"'

'[Which was] clever because he just turned me *inside out*.'

Once again Ramsay was taking a battering, but sucking in the energy from each blow and using it to fuel his growth as a chef. The fastidious culture of Le Gavroche meant that the necessarily more *laissez-faire* habits that he brought from Harvey's were unacceptable and he was constantly threatened with the sack for being untidy or, worse still, trying to help somebody else out. 'I'd see another section in the kitchen going down and I'd be ready, boxed off, I couldn't stand still so I'd jump on there ... [They'd] pull me out and say, "It's f***ing dog eat dog in here. You stay away from that section!"'

The Saturday-night moonlighting at Harvey's came to an end when Michel Roux Jr discovered what was going on and became upset – once again it was a question of allegiance. Ramsay, at his own request, then took on the job of night baker at Le Gavroche, not a highly prized position given that you started at midnight and worked until midday. His superiors could only ask why, but it was a maverick step that signals much about Ramsay's motivation at that time. His reasoning was simple: he needed to know how to make bread. At this point there was no great game plan to rise up through the ranks and reach the top of the profession, but he was ravenous in his appetite for learning. He'd fallen in love with food and that was motivation enough.

'I didn't feel like King Dick but what I did do is I just rose to the challenge. That was my section and no one was ever going to run that section. I didn't want to go on holiday, I didn't want to do outside events, I didn't want to be away from it. My marbles [for filleting fish] were all broken and every morning I used to take pleasure in putting it together … I can't say that I knew I was good, but I was on a mission … a big, big mission. I just got better and I got intimidated by nothing and everything I saw from a salsify, to a fresh sturgeon, to albino caviar, just mind-blowing stuff … [I was] just obsessive.'

Fortunately, Le Gavroche was an obsessive's paradise. The commitment to quality and consistency was executed with a ruthlessness that has left an indelible mark on Gordon Ramsay. Absolutely nothing left the kitchen unless it was precisely as it should be. Early one morning he had a problem with the bread and, pushed for time, drastically abbreviated the intricate process for making *sablé* biscuits. Albert walked in and caught him red-handed. 'It was about ten past five and there was this slap, right on the back and it was Albert and he said to me, "Leave it. Leave it! Don't touch that, leave it." And he made me leave it there until seven thirty when Michel came in to see what I'd been doing, that he'd caught me. And I got pummelled ... absolutely pummelled. So I learned then that he didn't get where he did by letting me take shortcuts. It was a massive learning curve, in the sense that they may have been in the shit, but they'd much rather have taken the dish off for lunch rather than have it done incorrectly.'

Although the hierarchy at Le Gavroche were quick to crack down on his indiscretions it soon became clear that they appreciated his talents. His commis status didn't last long and he was given the fish section to look after. The periodic efforts to cut him down to size are evidence of the high regard in which he was held – it was essential that he didn't get ahead of himself and that he understood how much he still had to learn. Le Gavroche was teaching him personal discipline and, crucially, how to marshal a large brigade in a fine-dining kitchen. And, while discipline was tight and the sanctions harsh, these went hand-in-hand with a strong dose of paternalism.

'I miss Gavroche ... for the safety it gave you ... the security. Marco cared about you, there was no two ways about it, but you never knew. You were on that edge. It was like sitting with your pants down on a meat cleaver dealing with Marco, because you never knew how quickly he was going to slice your arse off. But at Gavroche you just felt so comfortable, it was a different mannerism.'

Ramsay had a problem with tax, a hangover from his time at

Harvey's. Michel Roux Jr found out and wrote him a cheque. '[He said], "Let me lend it you. Get rid of the worry. Stay focused, don't let it disrupt you."' It was a crucial time for Ramsay, who had been asked to go to Hotel Diva in the French Alps where Albert had a consultancy arrangement, and he didn't need any additional worries hanging over him. As it was, he departed solvent, with the benefit of Albert's blessing and under his belt the experience of working in both the hottest kitchen in Britain and the most revered. He also had barely a word of French. So endowed, he headed off across the Channel with the last stage of his apprenticeship about to begin.

The five months at the Hotel Diva were to be a precursor to the more serious task of working for Guy Savoy in Paris. It would give the 23-year-old the opportunity to learn something of the language and acquaint himself with the Gallic way of doing things before he was thrown in at the deep end in the French capital. As it transpired, working at a ski resort would also prove to be something of a breather from the breakneck pace he had experienced at Le Gavroche and Harvey's. Mastering the slopes presented Ramsay with a challenge outside the kitchen and it gave him an opportunity he could only have dreamt of a few years before – skiing trips were never likely to figure on the list of holiday options for the hard-pushed Ramsay family. The pattern of work at Diva meant he could ski during the day and be in the kitchen at night. 'It was like having fifteen years of skiing holidays compressed into five months,' he recalls.

If the French culture and ski resort lifestyle were something of a revelation, his time at Hotel Diva was to be a turning point in a much more significant way. It was here that the realisation came that he had the resources to reach the top of the profession. He had been transported this far courtesy of a greedy appetite for knowledge and a dogged determination to rise to any challenge put before him. Satisfying his wide-eyed curiosity and taking pride in his refusal to be bowed by whatever was thrown at him, had been ends in themselves. Since he started cooking he'd been head down, concentrating on the road immediately ahead. Now, for the first time, he let his eyes lift to the horizon.

'The maître d' there was Jean Claude [now restaurant manager at Restaurant Gordon Ramsay] ... he said, "You know last night on your night off ..." I said, "Don't tell me ... chef went down?" He said, "No, no, no, the chef didn't go down. All the customers were asking, is it the chef's night off?" and that made my day ... just told me that, hey, I *can* do something ... and oh that was it! That was the seed planted. I was thinking, hold on a minute, he's Albert's right-hand man and the customers are turning around and telling Jean Claude that the chef's off when [actually] he's on and it's *my* night off. And then things started to happen ...'

Strangely enough, what happened next was a competition. I say strangely because competition cooking is generally a pernicious influence on the quality of eating out. The process of a line-up of chefs cooking to impress a posse of portly judges seems to bring out the worst in them. It results in food that is intended to be looked at, dissected, prodded, perhaps photographed and finally, almost as an afterthought, tasted. It favours presentation over content, pretension over flavour and promotes culinary conceits like spun sugar cages and apples carved into swans. Simply put, it encourages dishes that are designed for many things – but being eaten is not necessarily one of them. None of this would be so bad if these traits were left behind in the exhibition halls that house the competitions, but they're not; the same individuals then go back to their restaurants and try to reproduce the same overblown style of cooking for seventy diners. I have eaten good meals by chefs who spend a lot of time cooking in competitions, but not many. If it is really necessary to turn cooking into a sport, I suggest breaking it down into individual disciplines and measuring speed rather than quality – peeling potatoes, filleting fish, dressing a crab, stuffing mushrooms. Put it in the Olympics. At least, then, nobody would be forced to eat the results.

Albert Roux entered Ramsay into the Chef of the Year competition at Olympia, sponsored by British Gas and organised by the Craft Guild of Chefs. He did the semi-final and won it but then had to wait a further year for the finals, by which time he was in Paris working under Guy Savoy, who had little regard for what he saw as something of an unnecessary indulgence. 'So I flew back the night before, got Steve Terry [a colleague from Harvey's] to do all the mise en place for me, did a trial at Gavroche. Albert went mad about me turning a crème brûlée out of the mould because it was a Guy Savoy crème brûlée and said, "Don't be so f***ing stupid, you never turn a crème brûlée out of the mould." So I went into it thinking, Oh my God, I've got bollocked. I took a little bit of Marco for the ravioli, I had the most amazing velouté of asparagus from Guy Savoy. I did the crème brûlée with two chocolates [and] Albert said, "It's f***ing stupid." He had a little office in Le Gavroche and he slammed the window over. So I was just thinking, f**k, it's too late now, my recipes are in, I've got to do this now, I can't change anything, I can't believe he's just said that to me the night before the competition. And I went in there and won it."

The lid was off. This was the first time that he had really cooked on his own and he was bursting with excitement at the liberation of cooking to his own agenda. The dishes weren't his but they were a microcosm of his experience so far, chosen by him and cooked by him. His success was an indication that he was no longer beholden to any individual style or regime. He was beginning to become the sum of those accumulated parts and, as the winning chef, for the first time Gordon Ramsay was becoming a name in his own right. 'I was twenty-five years of age and there was this chef de cuisine, that sous chef, this executive chef, every Tom, Dick and Harry, and there was me, Gordon Ramsay, on the brochure, *commis chef de cuisine Guy Savoy, Paris*, and so it was f***ing amazing. Two thousand pounds prize money, bits and bobs of publicity for British Gas, happy as Larry.'

His triumph wasn't going to cut much ice in Paris though. Guy Savoy was already a leading chef in France, part of the culinary elite, holding two Michelin stars and widely tipped to be the next to achieve the ultimate three. The pay was a miserly 3,900 francs per month (about £390) and the only other benefit of note was a contribution of 50 per cent towards his Metro ticket, so once again he resorted to working on his day off, this time at the Café Bastille making espressos and lattes – a task that he took typically seriously. 'My waiters look at me now when I get upset when I say it's not a latte because it's a cappuccino, they've taken the milk too far and you can't mix it so the milk stays on top of it and it's just sad. And they think I'm a f***ing lunatic but I know how to make a proper latte and I know how to make a cappuccino … Twelve quid on a Sunday to work a seven to three shift and that was my spending money.'

With this pitiful sum he would buy a telephone card and ring home, but the calls became less frequent as he immersed himself in France. Long distance was lengthening by the day as he disciplined himself to speak as little English as possible, listening to Linguaphone tapes on the way to work and eventually finding it hard to even summon up the English to speak to his mother. 'I knew I needed to learn and to get inside [their heads], I had to become French, and I did, I really did.'

There was something quite different about the French approach to food and cooking and he needed to understand that. But it wasn't something he could simply learn, he had to live it, so much of it seemed to come instinctively and he needed to absorb that instinct too. The love of great ingredients, respect for the seasons, passion for freshness and a refusal to tolerate poor quality seemed to run through their veins. Their understanding of the raw materials involved and how to appreciate their quality surpassed anything he had experienced before.

'The French are, rightly so, arrogant because they've got something to be arrogant about, in the sense that they are the creators, the masters. It's normal for them to sit around the table and have the most amazing choux farcie, casserole lapin, tarte tatin, beautifully done, and eat off the same plate. They don't have the etiquette about changing plates. They'll have their rabbit bones on there, a slice of brie and then they'll finish it with a tarte tatin on the same plate and eat off it without any airs and graces ... and so it was an amazing insight.'

Some aspects of French kitchen life were familiar enough though. Ramsay was still very capable of making mistakes, and early on in his time in France his mastery of the language was less than complete. The possibility of a slip-up was thus heightened and Guy Savoy wasn't about to make allowances. Ramsay took responsibility for signing in the delivery of *coquillage* (shellfish), and overwhelmed by the beauty of the bounty he had been presented with, started busily cleaning the clams – astounded by the variety he found in the sack.

'I was cleaning away and everyday at twelve o'clock Guy Savoy would arrive, he'd go straight to his notice board, pick up the phone, order a coffee. He was as grumpy as f**k and then he'd look for these certificates ... these certificates came stapled on the side of the net [that held the shellfish]. What I didn't realise was that I should have kept these things because if there was a trace of bacterial growth, food poisoning, they could go back and trace it instantly ... but of course they were in the bin. I got mullered, I got sent back down to the pastry, I got told to speak fluent French and I got told I had two weeks to learn, to understand, otherwise I could go to work in Hippopotamus [a chain brasserie] like the Aberdeen Angus Steak House.'

This was three months into his stint with Guy Savoy and he took it as a cue to redouble his efforts. He acquired a French girlfriend, refused to talk English with his French colleagues and, in his thirst for knowledge, worked in other kitchens in his time off. 'I was obsessed and I have to say near compulsive. I just didn't give a fig [for anything else], I used to go and spend days in different kitchens, where I'd got to know the chefs.'

It was a fertile environment in which to grow. After shifts it was common for chefs to pour out of their respective kitchens and congregate in the cafés. The talk was inevitably of food, ideas were exchanged, experiences shared. If Ramsay thought of himself as near compulsive then he was in good company and it was an indication that in this respect he had achieved his aim to 'become French'. 'I'd just never been anywhere so focused and obsessed with hitting perfection. So when people knock France now, *a* I daren't and *b* it gave me so much.'

He followed Guy Savoy with an eight-month spell at Jamin, where Joel Robuchon already held three Michelin stars. There he joined fellow Brits Michael Caines and Robert Reid in a kitchen that, courtesy of Robuchon's management style, was a reminder of Ramsay's days at Harvey's ('but ten times worse'). By then though he was becoming much surer of his own abilities, and armed with fluent French and the responsibility of running a section, he was able to start dishing out a little bit of what he himself had taken by the bucket-load. 'It was hard, but I could stand alone then. I could put my spikes out in French, I could rip into the apprentice, I could rip into the chefs de partie and I could give a little bit of British beef back.'

Some of Robuchon's dishes came as a surprise to Ramsay. The likes of ravioli of langoustine, wrapped in a Chinese paste with cabbage and foie gras sauce were as sophisticated and delicate as any cooking he had seen, but they were in the company of much simpler dishes such as deep fried *merlan* (whiting) served with maître d'hotel butter and lemon. 'I didn't understand it, it didn't balance. But then it was *the best* deep-fried *merlan*, the best butter, filleted to order, it [had] arrived that morning and it was fresh oil every time we cooked it. So I started to realise … Jamin gave me the balance of the different diversities.'

This is a necessary revelation that comes to all the best chefs at one time or another – that often it's the simple things that are the best and can't be improved on. By their nature and training, chefs are naturally inclined to want to work on their food – after all that's their job. To have the confidence and understanding to keep it simple is a rarer skill, to resist the temptation to go one flavour too far, to be prepared to let the food speak for itself – that is a real talent. And only the best chefs have it.

That's not to say that the more technically complex dishes aren't worth the effort. The langoustine ravioli, for instance, sounds to me like an astounding, inspired dish. Even more so when you take into account that, unbelievably, the shellfish themselves are cooked to the customer's requirements in the way usually reserved for red meat – something that requires an astonishing precision. Ramsay got it wrong, served the *bien cuit* (well done) before the *saignant* (rare) and allowed the foie gras sauce to split on a plate that was too hot. The dish, rejected on the pass, was returned to him through the air, the whole plate crashing into his ear and leaving a luxurious mess of langoustine and foie gras sauce dripping down the side of his face – a criminal waste.

France had one last gift for him before he moved on. He secured a month's *stage* (a temporary placement) with Alain Ducasse at Louis XV in Monaco. It was a fine and fitting conclusion to his French odyssey and led to an unlikely but timely stint as chef on Australian media mogul Reg Grundy's yacht – complete with on-board helicopter, Porsche and Harley Davidson – which was moored in Monte Carlo. It was a chance opportunity prompted by a conversation with a girl in a bar, but it proved to be just the break that was needed.

'What it did do was charge my batteries ... Perfect ... Boy, I needed time out, mentally, I'd gone through the biggest headf**ck of training that one could ever hope to do in such a short period of time.' Ramsay's job was simply to cook for the owners and their guests – the crew had a separate chef – but as they were rarely on board it was an invitation to relax, soak up the sun and take in the delights of the various ports of call. He ran, swam and, while the other crew members went off to play golf, head inland to eat at the local restaurants, learning about regional cooking in Corsica, Sardinia and mainland Italy. It was all 'money in the bank' stored away for future reference. The work was limited and the crew, used to having extravagant leisure time and the vessel to themselves, seemed to almost resent it when the owners were on board. Much as he needed the break – and if he'd known what was coming he might have valued it even more – Ramsay began to feel ill at ease with the comfort zone he found himself in. The cosseted lifestyle was seductive and he feared complacency. He also felt pangs of guilt at the lack of effort required from him in return for the lifestyle. Despite an offer from the Grundys to set him up in a restaurant in Sydney – 'My fear of going to Sydney, at the age of twenty-six, was never coming back … it's such a draw, you don't have to work very hard, there's more talent there' – he headed back to the UK, stiffened by his experiences and simmering with ideas. Base camp had been established, now he was set for an attempt on the summit.

The final ascent was to prove steeper and more furious than he could possibly have imagined. Initially he took a reasonably conventional route, securing the job of head chef at Pierre Koffman's Tante Claire, a legend among London restaurants and holder of three Michelin stars. Koffman's regime came as something of a surprise, out of kilter with the rigorous attention to detail that he'd been used to in France, at

Le Gavroche and at Harvey's. 'I wasn't used to that set-up ... not because I came back all swanky and snobby ... Koffman was the most amazing guy with flavours and the execution side was never his forte, it was very rustic. I suppose the shock horror was that he didn't want to invest in non-stick pans, he didn't want all the stoves on because of the gas bill, he had all the kitchen lights out and the restaurant lights out in the afternoon and all the fish came on a Wednesday and then got prepped up and put on ice. He was totally oblivious at midday to what would be on the lunch menu ... so many miles away from what I'd experienced.'

Nevertheless the pay, at £500 per week, was in a different league from what he had been used to and this was the chance to bank another priceless experience – heading up a team for the first time. Doing a stint here would further enhance his reputation and prepare him for future challenges, perhaps even his own restaurant, maybe in a year or two.

It lasted three months. Marco Pierre White had other ideas for Ramsay's future. He had followed up Harvey's with a second triumph at the Canteen in Chelsea Harbour and he was about to move his set-up into the Hyde Park Hotel, the perfect venue to make a bid for his missing third star. From his experiences at Harvey's, White was well aware of Ramsay's prodigious energy and his natural talent. It was an injection that Tante Claire needed and with hindsight Ramsay suspects that this was troubling his former employer and prompted him to act – '[It was] the fact that I'd gone to Tante Claire, that he was about to move Harvey's into the

Hyde Park Hotel and he didn't want me reviving [it] and putting all this energy into Tante Claire.'

With no hint of any ulterior motive White took Ramsay to a restaurant called Rossmore, a fine-dining venue that was experiencing some difficulties. Ramsay was taken with the place and told Marco so. 'He said, "Yeah, but it needs this and it needs that." Strangely, when it came to the bill, Ramsay discovered there wasn't one and at this point he learned that Claudio Pulze, White's partner in the Canteen, was the part owner. 'We got outside and Marco said, "Would you like it?"' This wasn't in the script. Ramsay had no capital to speak of and the job at Tante Claire was providing him with an income that he could only have dreamt of months before. A share in his own restaurant with complete control of the kitchen was not yet a serious possibility, not even a twinkle in the young chef's eye. Yet in an instant, without warning, it was a sudden reality. Aubergine was about to be born.

☆☆☆

How many really good managers are there in any field? Not that many. It's easy to be a bad manager. Just look at the options: you can be one of those who don't give a damn one way or the other, someone whose only motivation is to cover their own backside, someone who expends all their energy and wastes everyone else's playing office politics, someone who is preoccupied by building their own sad little empire in a seventeen-storey office block. You can be too soft, you can be too hard.

Gordon Ramsay's management style has attracted its share of censure: 'Absolutely atrocious' ... 'Obsessed' ... 'Manic' ... 'Obsessive' ... 'Nasty' ... 'Vicious'. Fellow chefs, former employers, directors of catering colleges, commentators in the press; just about everyone has had a go at one time or another – but these aren't their comments. They're Gordon Ramsay's.

All the above adjectives are packed into a single sentence in reply to a small enquiry I make about his management skills at the time he took on Aubergine. He has his head bowed and he's speaking slowly, in a hush. It's not that he sounds ashamed, just resigned, a little regretful and for the first time in our conversation, somewhat weary.

Aubergine opened in October 1993. For the first time Ramsay set himself a very clear target for the future; his aim was to 'replicate Harvey's'. Not in terms of attempting to reproduce the cooking style, the restaurant design or even the excitement that surrounded Marco Pierre White and his exploits. The ambition was very specific: to reproduce Harvey's meteoric success with Michelin inspectors and quickly achieve a first star before moving to two within a further two years. Three stars in two years – that was to be the mantra. The first guide would be out in January 1994, too soon to accrue the necessary number of inspections for a star. January 1995 was a more realistic target, but a tough call nevertheless. Some chefs wait a decade for their first star. Some chefs wait in vain.

He wasn't just competing against the clock; the field was becoming ever more crowded. He was part of a new generation of chefs that were coming through to challenge the old guard in the shape of the Roux brothers, Koffman and Raymond Blanc. Besides the Canteen, there was a flurry of excitement around Rowley Leigh at Kensington Place, Simon Hopkinson at Bibendum, David Cavalier at Cavalier's, Richard Corrigan at Fulham Road. Even in this company Aubergine quickly started to gather momentum. Whenever London's best fine-dining restaurants were listed, Aubergine was there in the company of Le Gavroche, Marco Pierre White at the Hyde Park Hotel, Nico Ladenis. Being associated with these names was clearly pleasing – but it wasn't enough. 'We were always sixth or seventh down the list. We didn't get a look in, but we were just bracketed with them … on the outside looking in. Knocking, knocking, knocking. Taking the panes of glass out of the door to get in, and I was just obsessed with getting in there.'

If Ramsay had learned anything through his experiences it was that he wouldn't achieve his goal by accident. He had seen the levels of intensity needed, the unyielding commitment to quality, the relent-less rhythmic consistency, the refusal to accept the slightest flaw, the intolerance of imperfection. He was completely aware of what was necessary and he knew only one way to get it.

'I didn't let anything go … I learned a lot. I feel I lost a few good staff through my own arrogance. And I can turn around and say that, not comfortably, but I suppose with a lump in my throat, because I wish they were with me now, because they're part of the success.

And if only they'd given me a little bit more time to show them the journey and what it was about ...'

The 1995 Michelin guide duly brought the first star but there was to be no relaxing. Ramsay was unceasing in demanding higher and higher standards from the team. They were working in the difficult, cramped conditions of a basement kitchen, a hothouse, in a team that included many of those whom Ramsay still surrounds himself with, including Marcus Wareing. Ramsay's dedication to the restaurant was singular whatever was occurring on the outside. 'I separated from my fiancée, my little brother started his addiction with heroin but the whole thing was so work orientated. I wouldn't pick up awards ... I wouldn't give the kitchen breathing space. Marcus used to get incredibly ... not pissed off, but I used to be breathing down their neck and I was adamant [for example] that the ravioli were made with the most transparent pasta and *everything* was done to such perfection.'

Maintaining those standards, retaining staff willing to put up with such hardships and keeping the whole thing together is a tall order. The challenge is to keep it up long enough to achieve the objective. For the staff it's always jam tomorrow and the whole thing will stay on the rails only if they remain persuaded that success is just around the corner. Just like at Harvey's, the chefs needed to feel they were part of something special, they needed to believe, to keep the faith.

What makes it all the harder is the mystery that surrounds Michelin. There are no set criteria to work to and there is no way of knowing quite where you stand in relation to their expectations for the various levels of award. The 1996 Michelin guide came and the single star was retained. It's a reasonable assumption to make that even if the cooking at Aubergine had reached the two-star level, the extra award would have been held back for a year, just to ensure that the performance was going to be consistent. It's a reasonable assumption but you don't know. No indication is given as to how far away you are from an additional star or, alternatively, if you're in danger of losing the one you've got – it's not a consultative process, you're kept completely in the dark.

For these reasons the 1997 announcement was crucial. If the momentum was to be kept up the second star was needed. It would also mean that, in his mind, Ramsay would have matched the achievement of Harvey's. Through Christmas and into the New Year the speculation in the top kitchens is at its peak. The industry is awash with rumours, half-truths, conjecture, supposed inside information. 'Every December is hell's kitchen,' says Ramsay. 'Every kitchen in Britain goes through the motions on who's got it, who's up, who's down. Did you hear about whoever losing their third star, John Burton Race is going to get three stars, what do you think of Pied à Terre? Are they going to get two stars?'

The kitchen at Aubergine was a pressure cooker at the best of times, but in the run-up to the 1997 announcement it was ready to blow. A single star is an achievement – about seventy or so restaurants reach this mark in the UK – two stars is a move into the elite with just six or so holding the award at any one time. The word was that Aubergine was about to move up but that meant nothing until

Michelin made their judgement public at the end of January and confirmed the speculation. It was two stars in three years.

Now the heat was really on. Ramsay was in the big league and attracting a proportionate amount of attention. In 1993, at the Hyde Park Hotel, Marco Pierre White had become the first British chef to win three stars and, at the age of thirty-three, the youngest ever holder of the maximum award anywhere in the world. Ramsay was six years younger than him; if he could turn Aubergine into a three-star restaurant by 2000 he'd have replicated that record. But it wasn't to be, not at Aubergine at least. Ramsay's business relationship with his partners in Aubergine – Claudio Pulze and the Milan-born Giuliano Lotto – was deteriorating and led to an acrimonious dispute in 1998 that eventually resulted in Ramsay walking out and taking his entire team with him. Their destination was a familiar one – Tante Claire.

The Tante Claire site had been on Ramsay's mind for some time, particularly after his short spell as head chef. 'I wanted it to be mine, more than anything. That was always my perfect site, that was the gem. Wow, Monday to Friday, fourteen tables, forty seats. I thought, how do I get in this position? How do I have what this man has got?'

Although he was by then an established figure and a good bet for the future he wanted to be as independent as possible in his next venture and that was going to take a considerable financial effort. He sold his flat, making a good profit, and entered into a crucial business relationship with his father-in-law, Chris Hutcheson (he had married Tana in 1996), who acted as guarantor, persuading the

Bank of Scotland to loan him the remainder of the cash (despite their puzzled reaction to him closing on Saturdays).

Once again he had an autumn opening, which in this case meant that Michelin's inspectors would be immediately crawling all over the place to assess whether he should retain the two stars. The legal battle that resulted from his departure from Aubergine was hanging over him, with vast sums of money at stake. Just to pile on the pressure he had boldly named the new venue Restaurant Gordon Ramsay. Then his father, who had never eaten his food, died of a heart attack two weeks before he was booked in at the restaurant – 21 January 1999, the day the new Michelin guide was due to be launched. On top of all this, he agreed to let the cameras in.

Channel 4's *Boiling Point* documented the opening of the new restaurant and its early progress. It was to have a profound effect on both Ramsay's public persona and his immediate fortunes. Distilled from eleven months of footage, the documentary captured the fervour and shone a light into a dark world of which most viewers knew nothing. You sit in a swanky restaurant, it's all calm and decorum, smiles and smoothness, but behind the kitchen door is another universe.

Just consider the context. Service is concentrated into a couple of hours. In that time, you've got to get out forty or so meals, all served to the same exacting standard, with no advance knowledge of what the orders are going to be. At this level, almost everything is cooked to order. It's hot, intense and terrifyingly fast. There simply isn't the time for pleasantries, and as Ramsay is so fond of saying, it's a 'shitfight'. If someone makes a mistake there can be no 'Hey, let's sit down and discuss this, never mind, you'll get it right next time.' Next time could be too late. Everyone has to be on their toes all the time and you have to be able to take the stick, gather yourself and move on. The simple truth is, if you're not tough enough, you're not going to last.

Boiling Point brought Ramsay condemnation for his treatment of staff; much of it from within the industry, some of it from those he worked for. While he doesn't seek to excuse his behaviour, it's obvious that this galls him more than anything, and although he doesn't use the expression directly you feel that the word hypocrisy is not far from his lips. '[A top chef] jumps on [the bandwagon] and says, "Yeah, this is terrible, this is shocking" ... What was that guy like twenty years ago, carving his reputation out? The guy was a f***ing lunatic! We're all from lunatic asylums, but we never like to confirm which one we work for.'

But *Boiling Point* was to have more serious consequences than stirring up some carping in the industry. The 2000 guide was the crucial date for three stars to equal Marco Pierre White's achievement at the age of thirty-three and only five years on from his first star. It was widely expected, but Ramsay was to be disappointed and he has no doubts as to why. 'Television ... I would have got that in five years, in 2000. I had an amazing meeting with Michelin, they expressed the complaints and they made it quite clear that I had exposed them.' An episode of *Boiling Point* had captured Ramsay uncovering a Michelin inspection in advance. 'I got told that there was a booking, it was from the head office in Paris and I obviously clicked that it was for Michelin.'

The episode meant a further, tense twelve-month wait before the next opportunity to reach his goal and it resulted in some soul-searching too. 'I was gutted when I didn't get my three stars because I really expected it. I contemplated Le Gavroche, Jamin, Marco had three stars by then, Nico and I thought, what am I doing wrong? But I wasn't *doing* anything wrong it was *me*! ... It was my father-in law, Chris, who said, "Can I have a word ... I don't mind running this and doing that but stand back and have a good look at yourself and just listen to yourself."'

Ramsay took stock, put his disappointment to one side and collected himself for one further push. 'You can't give up. Because I've had so many hurdles. I mean we didn't start off with any of this, this was not *given* ... on a f***ing silver spoon, so the total appreciation is ten times better because you've come out of the ground from a f***ing seed.'

One year later Ramsay is told there are two men to see him in the bar of his restaurant. A pair of Dereks – Brown and Bulmer – from Michelin. They are there, they say, to talk to him about the rumours that he has won three stars in the forthcoming publication of the guide. '[They said] "We're here to confirm that you *have*." It was like *my God*!'

'It was a complete weight off my shoulders. It was like represent-ing your country, and it was like climbing Everest and getting to the very top and letting out the biggest scream. But what I *couldn't* do was let off! I couldn't say anything and I gave them a big handshake and well ... you don't cuddle the Michelin inspectors, they're not there to be cuddled. I just wanted to go through and scream but I had to sit there for another fifteen or twenty minutes and discuss the ins and outs of the young cooks in Britain today and it was like f**k! I want to go! Let me explode! And I went through to the kitchen and the guys just rejoiced. It was like winning the FA Cup and the Premier League all in one!'

Or perhaps more like an Olympic Gold for the marathon, because this was a hard-won individual achievement. Ramsay hadn't started out with a three-star dream – if anything he had begun with a literal vision of that FA Cup and Premier League double (or at least the Scottish Cup and Scottish League double). The love of food wasn't in his blood, it got in there like a virus born in the atmosphere of the places where he worked. Places where reverence and respect for the best things that grace our tables infected the very air that he breathed. It was a relationship that grew over time and it was a love that came in tandem with lust, a fierce desire to meet the challenges thrown up by this extraordinarily demanding world, to stand up to each new trial, defy expectation and move on energised, to the next test.

A trio of asterisks in a little red book represented the culmina-tion of more than a decade of toil and extraordinary dedication and, to him, it felt like nothing ever had or ever will. 'I've never been present at my wife's [giving] birth, because I can't really go through that trauma because I hit a massive point in being told that I've got three stars and I never, ever want anything to affect that. That's what it meant.'

The summit can be a confusing place to be. You've worked so hard to get there, hacking and scrambling your way up the face, that you almost become defined by the climb, you become a mountaineer but quite suddenly there's no mountain. Before you is the prospect of a fall, in the distance other quite different mountains. For Ramsay there was a precedent. A precedent set by the man whose path had been so similar, who had faced comparable obstacles, surmounted them to reach the top and come face to face with the same stark question.

On New Year's Eve 1999 Marco Pierre White hung up his apron for the last time. He too had stood at that pinnacle and contemplated the question posed by the precipice before him. His answer was to make it disappear. He would no longer be cooking and therefore his cooking could no longer be judged. In advance of leaving the stove, he 'handed back' the three stars that Michelin had bestowed upon him. It was a gesture made in fantastic defiance of the abstract – there is no certificate, no trophy that comes with Michelin's approbation, there was nothing to return. You don't hold these stars any more than you can grasp the light of the ones in the night sky. But the deed served its purpose; he had voluntarily kissed them goodbye, they hadn't and couldn't be taken away.

White was already seeking challenges elsewhere. By the time he stood down he was already overseeing a small empire of excellent restaurants that suggested he might succeed in his avowed intention of reaching the same status as a restaurateur as he had achieved as a chef. Restaurants such as Quo Vadis in Soho and the Criterion in Piccadilly were, for a time, brilliant reflections of the White genius that was still on first-hand display at the Oak Room. Not mirror images in any way but possessing the same attention to detail, the same striking depth of flavour, the same reworking of classic dishes giving them a life and a vibrancy they'd rarely displayed, the same bloody-minded refusal to compromise on quality. The realm expanded to take in the glamour of Mirabelle, rapidly followed by Drones, Bentley's and Wheeler's. All were legends of the London restaurant scene but they were also tired old timers living on their past. White would come along, dispense his own brand of Viagra and in no time at all they'd be on their feet again, rejuvenated, bursting with a new lease of life.

It was an inspired episode but rolling out restaurants in this way, at this pace, is a notoriously difficult trick to pull off and these weren't restaurants in the business of being mediocre or adequate, or serving a purpose, they were about being exemplary. Other projects came in quick succession but there seemed to be an increasing tendency for them to burn brilliantly at the start and then begin to flicker and fade before in some cases being extinguished altogether. There were other ventures around the country such as lending his name to the restaurants of a few spanking new five-star hotels. Typically, they started off all right but seemed to quickly ebb away into ordinariness until the only thing left of the great chef was his name on the menu.

The latest edition of *Harden's London Restaurants* still includes Quo Vadis and you can take your pick of 'totally gone downhill' or 'routine and ordinary' from among the reader comments. The Criterion arguably fares worse – choose from 'really second-rate food' or 'the most arrogant and ill-mannered service in town'. Mirabelle finds a little more favour for its 'fantastic' wine list, 'attentive' service and 'timeless catalogue' of French cuisine, but even then many found it 'uninspired'.

It's only a guidebook, but there was a time when if someone had said that about a restaurant that Marco Pierre White had put his name to I'd have wanted to punch them. It doesn't make any sense I know, but all I can tell you is that this man did heroic things with food. In fact when Michael Winner calls a dish *historic*, as he often does, it actually makes adjectival sense when I think of MPW's food. It did indeed make history, not just because he was the youngest chef to get three stars, but because his cooking marked a time when he was serving up better food than just about anyone else in the UK had done before and because his influence at that time has changed so many things for the better.

I don't really have any right to be pissed off about this. The man owes us nothing and he already did us the great favour of serving all that wonderful food in the first place. It's just ... well, it's just a bit like Welsh rugby. Once there was magic and now it's gone and its current parlous state is in danger of casting a dismal mist over the glory days. However slim the likelihood, I live in hope that those days will return just like I live in hope that Marco Pierre White will one day put that apron back on.

And I'm not alone in that. 'I just wish, if I had one wish [it would be] that he was still cooking,' says Ramsay, 'because the guy could be up there with Alain Ducasse [among the most celebrated of French chefs and someone who has expanded his empire with remarkable success]. I've never been in competition with the Roux brothers, I've never been in competition with Marco White. I find it hard to get in competition with the people that taught me how to get where I am today. I don't pose a threat, I just see them making mistakes and me very happily tucked in behind, learning from their mistakes.'

☆☆☆

Ramsay may have learned from the experiences of others but this has scarcely deterred him from launching out on adventures of his own. There have been more restaurants and now, of course, there is television. Many more people will have seen the increasingly common appearances of the man on our screens than will ever eat in one of his restaurants. Yet he seizes every opportunity to remind people that the whole sprawling enterprise is founded on what he achieved in the kitchen. His frequent rejection of the label 'celebrity chef' may seem laughable to some and it can look as though he's trying to have his cake twice, but when you examine how he arrived at this point it's not hard to see why the moniker irks him. Perhaps it would be more accurate to describe him as a 'chef celebrity' – the distinction may seem a semantic one but for someone who has lived it, it couldn't be more real.

Alongside the media onslaught, the business of serving food has continued. Ramsay has surrounded himself with a team of key chefs whom he feels he can rely upon. Many of them have already made a name for themselves in their own right, most notably Marcus Wareing. Gordon Ramsay at Claridges under Mark Sergeant has its own Michelin star as does Angela Hartnett's restaurant at the Connaught. Jason Atherton is garnering plenty of acclaim at Maze in Grosvenor Square. There is also the Boxwood Café at the Berkeley Hotel, a more relaxed operation in the self-professed style of an upscale New York café.

And then there was Amaryllis, which ultimately didn't succeed because, as Ramsay admits, its upmarket, fine-dining formula just wasn't sustainable in the area. That area, oddly, was Glasgow the very city where he experienced the piercing disappointment that sent him careering off into a quite different profession.

Quite different, but with conspicuous similarities too. Ramsay has achieved far more in the kitchen than he had achieved in football or was realistically likely to. While success in both football and cooking require their share of hard work to go with the talent, the balance in the kitchen is much more heavily weighted towards graft. Gordon

Ramsay's tale is one of phenomenal commitment and it's a commitment born of passion.

'You're impregnated … and the day it's not there I want to stop. But I'm thirty-seven, I've got another fifteen or twenty years and I'm on top of my game … I've got out of the struggle and the shitfight is over.'

HESTON BLUMENTHAL

The Curious Case of Heston Blumenthal

I was clinging on to Christmas. In a couple of days it would be New Year and that would be an end to it. Christmas Day was fast retreating into the past and the tide of excitement was ebbing away at a noticeably quicker rate than it had rumbled in prior to the 25th. At seven years old I was already a veteran of festivities, experienced enough to know the value of stretching the anticipation as far as possible beyond the frenzy of Christmas morning. Very deliberately, I had rationed the few nuggets of novelty still to be uncovered – an Airfix plane ready for assembly, a plastic sword waiting to be unsheathed and, especially, a shiny red electric train yet to leave the station …

…and fated never to depart the sidings. Cogs, flywheels and axle pins were scattered among the carpet pile, many half-hidden and destined for the Hoover. The fire-red plastic carcass of the locomotive lay on its side, empty. In the centre of my bedroom my small friend sat cross-legged, head bowed, fixated on the brassy cylinder that he held in his hands. 'I think this is the engine,' he said without looking up, his tiny thumbs straining to prise apart the final recalcitrant pieces.

It was my own fault, I should never have left him alone in there. He had previous on this kind of thing, a substantial track record. Under my bed was a box crammed with the scrap of his previous dissections – an action man without limbs, a useless convoy of trucks with no wheels, an arsenal of mini armaments rendered harmless. It wasn't that he was destructive, just fanatically curious. The following Christmas I was given a hamster, but he'd left the village by then.

I've never been that inquisitive. Maybe the activities of my childhood acquaintance have left their scars – the disappointment of seeing so many treasured possessions wrecked in the name of a questioning mind may have left me wary. More likely, it's an inherent laziness and complacency. My parents once bought me an enormous hardback book called *How it Works*. Lavishly illustrated and detailed, it explained the science behind hundreds of everyday items from packet soups to pinball machines. I flicked through it once and never went there again. How does it work? Who cares? As long as it functions, that's good enough for me. It's a rubbish attitude really, little more than indolence and a willingness to rely on other people who have acquired the skills I couldn't be bothered to learn. But there is another side to it – I like to preserve the magic too.

The temptation
To take the precious things we have apart

To see how they work
Must be resisted, for they never fit together again.

The songwriter Billy Bragg said that, and he's seldom wrong about these things. Whether it's music or art, literature or love, there's always someone out there aching to deconstruct it for us, strip it down to its component parts and leave the carcass lying on the carpet. Maybe I'm just a hopeless romantic, but I believe in retaining some mystery, a sense of wonder. All this eagerness for enquiry, this fever to find out, it's just alien to me.

Heston Blumenthal is one of the most enquiring people I have ever met; he burns with curiosity. He is not, however, an alien, although you could perhaps be forgiven if his name led you in that direction. In Douglas Adams's *The Hitchhiker's Guide to the Galaxy* the lead character is a visitor to Earth from a planet in the vicinity of the star Beetlegeuse. In the naïve belief that it will help him blend nicely into the local culture, he takes the name of a once popular car and henceforth is known as Ford Prefect. No more than a medium-sized contraflow system from Blumenthal's Berkshire restaurant there is a much patronised motorway service station that goes by the name of Heston – well, it does make you think.

It's easy to make the wrong assumptions when you've little more than a name to go on. When I first heard of Heston Blumenthal it was as a bit-player in a supposed spat involving Marco Pierre White and Gordon Ramsay. Marco had turned up for Sunday lunch at the Fat Duck, Heston's Berkshire restaurant, to find Gordon already seated on the terrace, enjoying the sun. Apparently displeased by the presence of Ramsay – whose star was then rising at an exponential rate – White asked the chef/owner to eject him from the restaurant. To avoid a scene, Ramsay departed quietly, taking the moral high-ground with him. The story, perhaps as intended, got national press coverage.

Reading all this at the time, I started to wonder about Blumenthal. He was obviously doing something right if his restaurant was being patronised by White and Ramsay. His name conjured up something exotic, possibly Eastern European? Nordic? Dutch? In Bath there was a celebrated chef by the name of Martin Blunos, of Latvian extraction. He sported a ponytail and an exaggerated droopy moustache. My mind made a connection, and I pictured Blumenthal as similarly hirsute, perhaps white-haired, certainly portly. His Bray restaurant, with its sunny terrace, was clearly an extravagant venue on the banks of the Thames, with a spacious kitchen and an army of well-drilled chefs, just like Michel Roux's nearby Waterside Inn.

Heston Blumenthal was, in fact, born in Berkshire. His father hails from Cambridgeshire and his mother from Essex. Somewhere there is a pipette full of South African blood but he reckons it is 'less than 1 per cent'. His other love besides cooking is martial arts. He goes to the gym most days and looks strong and solid. He has no facial hair and the closely shaved fuzz that adorns his head has a reddish hue. His restaurant is on the side of the main road; it is small and understated. The kitchen, though now extended, is still tiny. As you can tell, I have an instinct for these things.

☆ ☆ ☆

Elsewhere in this book there is talk of the last-resort nature of a job in catering in the UK, how even some of the very best chefs came to the profession from an arid desperation, a dearth of alternatives. Steadily seduced by the aromas of the kitchen, the adrenalin rush of a busy service, the simple beauty of good ingredients, a passion develops and intensifies into an obsessive affair. What starts out as necessity, gradually develops over time into real desire. But that's not the case here, this story is different. For Heston Blumenthal, it was love at first sight.

They met by chance. Oustau de Baumanière is a long-fêted Provençal restaurant with rooms. An *oustau* is a local term for a village house, and this one dates from the fourteenth century and has the simple rustic charm that is easy to find in this part of France. The backdrop is of vales, olive trees, scrubland and vines. The dining room opens on to a terrace where you can eat when the weather is fair. These days the restaurant has two Michelin stars but when the fifteen-year-old Heston Blumenthal sat on the terrace it was one of the select few holding three. He came with his family on a pilgrimage from their London home, but the Blumenthals were no gastronomes. This wasn't a family who ate out regularly at classy restaurants; they'd never had the resources to do so for a start. Things had started to go well in his father's office equipment business and the visit to Ostau de Baumanière was a reward inspired by a piece of travel writing in a national paper. It was an almost random decision, a treat for the family and a beguiling twist of fate for the young lad whose only experience of eating out had been the occasional chicken in a basket and rare visits to a Berni Inn for duck à l'orange.

He clearly remembers it as if it had been yesterday. 'It was just such a shock. Sitting outside with the rocks lit up above, you could hear the crickets and smell the lavender and you had the sommeliers with their leather aprons, handlebar moustaches and enormous tastevins. The wine list seemed about four feet high. People pouring sauces into the lobster soufflé and the cheese trolley looked like a wagon. Carving stuff at the table ... even the noise of the feet on gravel ... I was knocked out by it ... Somehow then, it got under my skin.'

The taste of the food played little part in the enchantment. It was too far away from what he knew to even make much sense at this stage. The menu was enormous and cryptic, beyond the French there was another layer of code to be unpicked, the foreign language of *haute cuisine* with its grand-sounding sauces and lofty techniques that made sense only to the initiated. The whole offering was cocooned in the choreography of a graceful theatre and reverence that left the teenager wide-eyed. He was captivated.

For a while at least it was to be a secret affair. At fifteen an interest in cooking wasn't necessarily the kind of thing you talked about with your mates, but the seed had been sown. Blumenthal, like many a teenage boy before him, began to spend more time in his bedroom poring over glossy photographs and using a dictionary to decipher strange words that he hadn't come across before. At first glance, standard adolescent behaviour, but these weren't magazines hidden under the bed, they were cookbooks from the great chefs including *La Nouvelle Cuisine* by the brothers Troisgros. When he told me he read it at sixteen, this seemed remarkable enough in itself. But it got better:

sw: You managed to get the English translation?
hb: No, it was all in French.
sw: Impressive. You had fluent French at sixteen years old?
hb: No, I translated the whole thing, word by word.
sw: You did what?
hb: Using a dictionary. Word by word.
sw: You realise that isn't normal?
hb: (grinning): Yeah, I know but …

On the surface he was an archetype of male conformity, his most conspicuous enthusiasm being for martial arts. 'This was at the time when I went from karate to full contact and for most people that was what they knew of me. Cooking was still something that women did … it hadn't yet made that leap …'

It's true. This was a few years BF (before Floyd) when there was still something questionable about a man in the kitchen. Blumenthal couldn't stop himself though, the more he read, the more he wanted to know. The compulsion grew, and he began to take risks. Before long he was making furtive visits to butcher's shops – he liked to watch. 'That visit to Baumanière had walloped my senses. I read everything I could find, about food, restaurants, cheese, wine and I went to the places were they did the basic work, just to see how it was done. I just hated not knowing how something was done, I still do.'

The obvious place to learn was, of course, a restaurant kitchen, and at seventeen he took the bull by the horns and wrote to the top twenty restaurants in London and the surrounding counties asking for a job. It wasn't a boom time in the industry and he received only one reply, but that reply was from Raymond Blanc, chef proprietor of Le Manoir aux Quat'Saisons, already established among the leading kitchens in the country. The offer of a ten-day trial, with the prospect of a full-time job if things went well, was something of a coup. He entered expectant, eager to get cooking, but he was in for a shock. The hard work wasn't a difficulty, that's what he was there for and he was robust enough to cope with some of the more brutal aspects of kitchen life. 'There was a French/English divide in the kitchen and I was working with this French bloke. He said something to me and I threatened him, I'd been fighting as a sport for ten years so I had no reason to take any crap ... so I started on this bloke and then I heard a voice saying, "What are you doing over there? Come over here, you shouldn't be working with him, come and work with me," and so then I changed section, didn't ask anybody, just changed section and it was Marco, it was Marco who was saying come over here.'

Despite finding an ally and willing mentor in Marco Pierre White (he would continue to show an interest in Blumenthal for years to come), it soon became clear that he didn't fit in the commercial kitchen environment at that stage in his evolution. Through his reading, he knew plenty about putting together the kind of dishes that emerge from top kitchens. What he didn't know was that the recipes and the cooking are only a tiny part of the picture. The mechanics of getting that food to the customer hadn't really occurred to him; it involved heavy demarcation and an abundance of simple, repetitive jobs. And for the new boy that meant five hours of topping and tailing beans. 'That was the biggest shock ... I just assumed I would be doing more diverse things. Which made no sense, I mean how can you be? And then I had sort of assumed I'd see a dish through from beginning to end but you can't do that, it's about sections, a bit from here and a bit from there. But I hadn't stopped to think about that.'

He was offered the job and turned it down. 'I felt a bit weak in doing that but I just knew that this wasn't the right path for me. I wanted to jump that bit ...' It wasn't so much a setback as a confirmation of the road he needed to take. 'I never, ever wavered. After that night at Baumanière I could never think of anything else, nothing was going to overtake that desire, I just had a different agenda I suppose ...' By then he was clear in his mind that at some point he wanted to have his own restaurant. Le Manoir had dealt him a handy lesson. Restaurant cooking wasn't all about shaking pans over a hot flame, there was a whole other set of things he needed to learn, but for the time being he went back to concentrating on the food.

And back to the office. Working as a credit controller and then in repossessions, he put up with a nine to five routine that he found grindingly tedious but that had the benefit of leaving him abundant free time to fill with a mixture of martial arts, reading about food and experimenting at the stove. 'Outside of training, I didn't do anything else. I had no extra stuff to do outside work, the job didn't demand anything else. So I filled that time with reading, cooking and saving up to eat. Basically like a sponge, soaking up everything.'

As hobbies go, it was relatively cheap, which was a good thing because, although his pay was reasonable, he needed to save every penny he could. He was developing an expensive habit, a heavy addiction to the best restaurants in France – the kind of places that some of us might go to once in a lifetime – with among the most expensive food in the world. This is a good place to step back and remind ourselves of the context here. A man in his late teens and early twenties, from an ordinary upbringing with no particular affection for food in his family background, eating his way across France, working his way around all of the three stars and a hefty portion of the twos. 'My mates would go to the pub and maybe spend £25 on a Saturday night. But I wouldn't do that, I kept hold of the cash, always working towards those two weeks in France.' Not usual, is it?

That fortnight, packed as it was with lavish meals, ensured he had plenty to chew on until the next expedition. All the time he was making mental notes of the dishes put before him and his ability to distinguish tastes gradually developed. When he got home he recalled his travels not in photographs or video recordings but as flavour memories etched into his palate. He'd remember the best crème brûleé he'd eaten, an outstanding vanilla ice cream, the perfect chip, and then he'd set to work in his home kitchen using the taste blueprint that had so impressed him. 'I'd come home and make it over and over again, maybe thirty times, trying to re-create what I'd experienced. Yes, referring to recipes, but through trial and error, varying things to gauge the effect, trying to work out what was going on.'

It was an approach that would define his cooking, and one that marks him out from most of his peers. Once you're in a real commercial kitchen, tied to your workplace, working all hours, all your energies have to be directed at the job in hand. The information that comes to you is largely prescriptive – you make something this way and it will work. Gradually you assemble a repertoire of techniques, you have your tools and you put them to work, but you don't necessarily have to understand *why* they work. It's like being taught one of those card tricks that depend on counting the cards into piles and reassembling them in a certain order – carry out the instructions correctly and it always turns out right, but few of us have a clue as to why.

For someone as naturally analytical as Blumenthal, it's easy to see why an apprenticeship in a formal restaurant kitchen would have frustrated him, but his goal of becoming a chef was as clear as ever. He kept in touch with Marco Pierre White and Raymond Blanc (another chef without a conventional background in kitchens). White's advice was that he should forget being a chef and be a restaurateur instead. White was getting his first taste of the latter role at the Canteen, and after the sweat of Harvey's, the new venture had opened his eyes to the advantages of a less hands-on position. 'You don't want to do this,' he told Blumenthal bluntly. 'It's too bloody hard.'

Blumenthal wasn't dissuaded. 'I'd always wanted to do it, and anyway, I'd realised I couldn't do anything else. I wasn't money-oriented enough just to put up with something for the cash alone and I hated office work.' This wasn't a pipe dream, but he knew that if he was going to make it happen, there were cavernous gaps in his knowledge that he needed to address. He'd seen only a little of a kitchen at work and besides a basic accountancy course associated with his credit controller's job, he had only a vague idea of restaurant finances. Typically he took to books, the few that exist, on how to set up and run a restaurant, and he took a part-time course in restaurant management.

I don't know what they teach on those kind of courses, and I've never read one of those books. Maybe I should have. Because from what I've learned of running restaurants, I still feel I'm missing something

– let's call it the 'easy answer'. I'm not sure that Marco Pierre White was right in his advice, having the responsibility of ownership can be just as arduous as working in the kitchen and one of your biggest worries will always be getting the right chef and keeping him or her. Unless, of course, you do both jobs yourself, which has its advantages – primarily that at least you know your chef shouldn't be lacking in motivation and that the owner will have a full understanding of the difficulties of running a successful kitchen. Of course, it means twice the work too, or, more frequently, it means that some of the work just doesn't get done and because there is no option but to ensure that the food is ready, it's the management side that tends to get ignored. This, unfailingly, leads to the 'busy fool' syndrome: the place is packed, the food is good, all the customers love you, you get high on the adulation, everything's going great. And then the bank statement arrives, and you find you haven't made any money or worse still you're losing it.

My wife runs a restaurant, it's a good restaurant and it's busy. She makes money, but not a lot, and certainly not as much as those people think who come in and see the place bursting with bonhomie on a Saturday night. 'When are you retiring?' they ask jovially. 'Where's the Ferrari?' they joke. It's understandable really. The sums of money they hand over aren't insubstantial, all that's on view to the public is the prosperous side of things and from the outside it *can* look a bit of a breeze. There's a natural assumption that if the restaurant opens at 7 p.m., that is when the work starts and it finishes when the last meals go out at ten. Hardly. Where does the fresh bread come from, the ice creams, the tarts, the stocks for the sauces? When is the veg prepped, the fish cleaned and filleted, the meat boned out? You remember that heart-warming story about the old cobbler and those helpful elves who did all his work overnight? Well, the little people don't do catering.

The truth is, there's very little in the restaurant business financially. You pay your 17.5 per cent VAT, but because there's no VAT on the raw materials there's little you can claim back. It's highly competitive, the customers are notoriously fickle and business is notoriously sensitive to the general well-being of the economy. I know much of this applies to many other businesses too, but believe me, there are easier ways to make money.

The restaurants that succeed are rarely driven by money alone. I suppose you could cite McDonald's as an exception, but that depends on your definition of restaurant and McDonald's is outside of mine. The reality is, you have to love it. It's not an enterprise you can enter into grudgingly. It can take all your energy and most of your money as Heston Blumenthal was about to find out.

☆ ☆ ☆

Blumenthal married in 1989 and he and Susanna were soon joined in their small Beaconsfield cottage by a baby son. The small amount of capital they had was tied up in their house and it was this that was earmarked as the start-up money for a restaurant venture. They began by looking abroad, and specifically at South Africa. The £40,000 or so available to them wasn't a great deal in UK terms but in South Africa it represented a useful sum, especially given the preferential exchange rates offered by the Financial Rand to anyone investing in the country. Blumenthal's father had spent a period of his education in Cape Town and there were family contacts there too.

The project came close to fulfilment but the restaurant purchase fell through at the last minute and they decided to stay in Britain. Looking much closer to home Blumenthal began checking out properties in the area he knew best – Beaconsfield, Marlow and their surroundings – where he surmised there was the potential clientele to support the enterprise. Opportunities came and went, other proposed purchases fell through, and it was three years before he settled on a pub in the Thames-side Berkshire village of Bray.

Bray wasn't a village he was familiar with, but he knew it was the home of Michel Roux's triple-starred Waterside Inn, which sits there on the banks of the Thames. It's a sedate little village, with most of the construction dating from the sixteenth century, and the Fat Duck is a pretty but unassuming roadside building that could easily be mistaken for a domestic cottage. It's possible that you may also have heard of the Vicar of Bray or at least of the traditional folk song that celebrates him. His great achievement was to possess a chameleon-like ability to prosper despite the many political and religious changes that took place during his seventeenth-century tenure. He did this by unashamedly trimming his stance on any subject to suit the direction of the political wind of the day. In other words, as a politician, he was about four centuries ahead of his time.

On this occasion the sale went through and suddenly Heston Blumenthal had a restaurant. He still had no proper kitchen experience of any note, although he had prepared himself by doing a month-long stint at Marco Pierre White's Canteen. This had been prompted by a very specific worry that was clearly keeping him awake at night. 'The one bit I couldn't get was what happens when a check [order] comes in. So I went to the Canteen … they were doing 250 on a service, they'd have about six checks coming in at a time. I mean how on earth do you remember all that? Two days in there and it was done and by the end I could run a section. So that was fine, I had that sorted out now.'

If he had the impression that was the last piece in the jigsaw, he was in for a rude awakening. Everything was tied up in the Fat Duck. They had given up their home and the family had moved back in with Heston's parents. From living in their own home, with a routine based on his nine to five job they were now without a place of their own and his wife and children were about to start seeing a lot less of their husband and father. 'It was chaos, it was absolute chaos. We hadn't thought of so much, in our naïvety we didn't even think of the size of the kitchen [it was tiny]. It was such a change for the family, we had a second child by then and where it used to be me doing a steady nine to five, suddenly I was sleeping at work.'

The fact that he was working such long hours was not an indicator of instant success but more of a symptom of the shambles that he started out with. In the kitchen he was joined by his oldest friend, a son of acting parents Una Stubbs and Peter Gilmour. He had no cooking experience. 'He said, "We're like brothers, so it'd be a good laugh if we worked together." So I said, "Well all right then," so it was us with two people out front. Just the four in total.'

On the second day after opening, they almost went down to a trio. 'It was five thirty, maybe six and I went to light the oven … It was a little oven, the pub oven and as it turned out the thermocouple wasn't working so I went to get the matches and the phone went. I answered the phone, came back, struck a match, put it in and *booofff*, it knocked me off the floor and I landed on the fridge opposite. My friend just started laughing. I could smell the hair, and then the burning started, I burned my scalp and my face. We had twelve people booked, so I had to stop covers there. And so I had this bloke in the kitchen who hadn't cooked before, with me standing outside the kitchen with a bag of frozen peas on one side of my head and a bag of something else on the other, telling him when to pull things in and out of the oven.'

There was little time for sleep. Later this would be because the restaurant was getting busy and the need to watch costs meant that Heston carried out as much of the work as he could himself. At the outset it was nothing to do with business levels – 'It was ridiculous because in fact we were doing very few covers' – the sleep deprivation was much more a result of shambolic organisation and a crippling lack of experience than of a busy restaurant. He was climbing a steep learning curve and the effort was absolutely draining.

'I didn't have suppliers and ordering properly sorted and I didn't know about stuff like mise en place lists. We'd be running out of food and I'd end up having to nip to the shops.' Not so much of a hardship you might think, but going days at a time without sleep was leaving him disoriented and prone to mistakes. Mistakes that in turn generated yet more work. 'We needed something for the lunch service, I can't remember what, so I had to run off to Waitrose which was the nearest supermarket I could get to. I had this old Metro van that cost me a hundred quid, looked like it had been painted in emulsion, but it kept breaking down. So I borrowed my mate's car, I went to the shops, came back a bit pissed off with it all, did lunch and afterwards I looked and we needed more stuff! I couldn't believe it. So I got back in the car, went off to the shops again, got the stuff, opened the boot and realised I hadn't unpacked the first lot, it was still in there.'

Blumenthal reckons that this spiral of exhaustion persisted for the first three years. 'You'd get so delirious you would be trying to light the blowtorch by putting it under the tap, but under the *hot* tap, some strange logic said it had to be the hot tap. I remember one day looking down at a piece of cod I'd been trimming and seeing I'd cut it in to strips and triangles – I'd just fallen asleep with the knife in my hand but kept going.'

This was bound to put pressure on home life, especially as he hadn't really anticipated the demands that the restaurant would make. 'Susanna was amazing. If I'd had to deal with an ear-bending about the hours I was working on top of everything else, we'd never have made it. She's the single most important factor in what's been achieved. Incredibly, I'd told her I'd be able to take some weekends off, or at least Sundays. That was a dream world.'

But much of his dreaming was now reality. It had been a decade-long courtship since that warm Provençal evening at Oustau de Baumanière. Finally he was in his own restaurant and at last he was cooking for a living.

☆☆☆

His first menu wasn't going to set the culinary world alight. It featured dishes such as pea and savory soup, a foie gras parfait, salmon rillettes, steak and chips, lemon tart, jasmine crème brûlée and the obligatory chocolate tart. Starters were priced at four pounds, mains at ten and desserts at three. But while the dishes were familiar, the cooking wasn't without ambition. 'I was trying to take what I'd learned over the past ten years, which was basically French classic cooking, and I then took that information and those techniques and put them to French bourgeois cooking.'

Simply put, he was trying to bring some extra refinement to simple French country cooking, to tune the dishes up, perfect them using the skills he had discovered in his reading and, just as importantly, experimentation. By the time he opened the Fat Duck his routine for chips, for example, was already in place:

HOW TO COOK CHIPS LIKE HESTON
First cook the chips in water, until they're almost falling apart (this is a small window of opportunity), drain them off and then put them in the fridge.

When they're cold, cook them in groundnut oil at 130°c. Cook them until they take on a dried appearance on the outside, before they take on any colour (this is also a small window of opportunity). Then put them in the fridge again.

Finally cook them in the oil again (or kidney fat) at 190°c.

So they get cooked three times in effect. I've never understood why it's necessary to shampoo your hair twice, so I can understand if this seems a bit convoluted. Why bother? Well, if you like your chips soggy, don't. The whole point of this exercise is to ensure that the chips are crisp and fluffy and that they stay that way long enough to last through your meal. The reason why chips lose their crunch is ... Well, it's probably better if I let Mr Blumenthal explain ...

'The reason the chips lose their crunch is because you've got the mass of moist potato in the middle. As that heats up, the water turns to steam and the steam builds up pressure and goes from the inside to the outside. So what's happening is that when you take your chip out of the fryer it's hot, so the steam's going outwards and that moisture is hitting the crust on the chip. Then it starts to cool down, so then that moisture instead of sitting on the surface and evaporating is now actually being absorbed back into the chip. And the same thing happens with fat, as long as your chips are getting hotter all the time, the fat's not going to be absorbed because the pressure of the steam is going to stop the fat getting into it. As soon as the chip starts to cool down, that's when the fat starts to be absorbed.'

Got that? Good. But that's not the end of it. The triple-cooked chip trick (try saying that with a mouth full of French fries) may have been with him since the start, but he has continued to work on ways of refining the technique and specifically getting more moisture out of the chip. Among the possibilities explored have been pin-pricking (successful but a tad on the labour-intensive side if you're thinking of serving more than one chip per person), drying the chips between each cooking (also requires an army of chefs and tends to make the chips tough rather than crispy) and finally the current front-runner, desiccation (as in coconut), where you put the chips in a vessel with a pipe in the side and the moisture is pumped away. This apparently leaves the chips crunchy for about twenty minutes after cooking.

I'm sceptical about the last bit. I've eaten these chips – they're terrific – and I find it implausible that anyone has ever had the willpower to wait twenty minutes before eating the final one. But it's when he gets on to a subject like this, riding a tide of enthusiasm at what he's unearthed, that you start to understand the essence of this chef and how, in just seven years, he went from offering uncomplicated food in a former pub that he struggled to buy, to two Michelin stars and widespread recognition as the most innovative chef in the UK.

There, I said it, *innovative*. We've got this far and I haven't even mentioned the bacon and egg ice cream. That is partly because at this stage in the story, chronologically, it didn't exist, but it's also because the bacon and egg ice cream, and the sardines on toast sorbet, together with the snail porridge and, of course, the tobacco chocolates, not forgetting the white chocolate and caviar sweets, the red pepper lollipops – all these and more, well, they tend to give people the wrong idea.

And I just know that some of you are reading this and thinking, no. Sardines on toast sorbet, no. Snail porridge, *non*. Bacon and egg ice cream, *nein*. *Dim* red pepper lollipops (that's Welsh that one). I can understand that, I really can see where you're coming from, I appreciate your point of view … but I can't condone it though. You're wrong. But the problem is, ever since I first went to the Fat Duck I've been struggling to find a way to explain it. Believe me, I've tried. I've stood in the pub and been asked by mates who knew the job I used to do, 'Been anywhere good to eat recently?'

'Well, yeah, terrific actually, this place up the M4 in Berkshire, Bray, the Fat Duck.'

'What did you have?'

This is where I start apologising in advance. 'Well, it sounds bizarre, but it really isn't.'

'What?'

'Sardines on toast sorbet.'

'Yuuhhhhhrrkkk.'

'Snail porridge.'

'Get off!'

'But it's brilliant, really, and anyway it isn't all like that, there's some more familiar stuff on the menu, and I know it sounds weird but it works, it really does and … Well, you really have to go there …'

And I know they're not going to be convinced. Just like some of you are not convinced, most of you even. The only way to understand it *is* to go and try it. I've taken sceptics there and without exception they've come away as converts. So that's what I suggest: make a trip to Bray (well, book first) and have a meal at the Fat Duck and tell them I sent you. That way when I go next I'll probably get something for free too.

NOTE: I think at this point I should make it clear that I recommend you visit all the restaurants of the chefs who so kindly gave of their time to be interviewed for this book. After all, if this one sells, I might get to do another one and I don't want to hack anybody off.

You don't have to cook anything quite as revolutionary to upset the customers though. A new restaurant is almost always going to have its fair share of unhappy guests. It can be quite disheartening, but logically it's not something you should worry about too much.

It works like this. There are a variety of people out there with an assortment of tastes and their view of what constitutes a good dining experience will fluctuate wildly. For some it may be simply about quantity (I used to come across this when visiting the local pub in the days when I ran a restaurant. 'I enjoyed the meal at your place the other night Simon, yes, very nice … Had to have a sandwich when I got home mind'), for others it may just be about the style of the food,

('I don't like all that fancy stuff ... Can you do it without the sauce?'). The point is that when you first open, nobody has anything to go on, so it stands to reason that some people are going to turn up and it just isn't going to be what they want. If you've never experienced this phenomenon before it can be pretty disturbing and genuinely upsetting.

Heston Blumenthal's description of some of the customer feedback in the early days at the Fat Duck will resonate loudly with just about anyone who's opened a restaurant that aspires to do decent food. 'We had the usual problems. "My fish isn't cooked enough, my food's not hot enough, where's my side dish of vegetables." [But] as we progressed, we were continually finding new sets of customers, alienating the old ones, finding new ones and taking some of them with us. And there's no getting around that.'

It can be a lonely and troublesome experience. This was a very self-contained operation and there was little in the way of advice coming from anyone outside the business. Marco Pierre White offered various bits of guidance which, in retrospect, Blumenthal wishes he'd taken more heed of ('It might have saved me a lot of grief'). Bookings soon accelerated though, perhaps helped by a well-meaning but typically bullish intervention by Marco. 'He rang me up and said "I've done some good publicity for you," so I thought, oh good, and then he said, "Yes, it's the biggest attack I've ever made on another chef."'

Marco had launched an assault on the Waterside Inn and specifically Michel Roux, employing the unlikely vehicle of an interview with the mighty *Maidenhead Advertiser*. 'He said something like "The sooner Michel Roux and his Waterside Inn fall into the Thames the better." I think he said, "Time isn't on his side,"' Blumenthal recalls, 'and "my friend Heston is going to do this and that". He was like "Isn't it great that I've done that!"'

Blumenthal had been in the village about three weeks at the time and picking a fight with the neighbouring restaurant, which just happened to be one of the most celebrated in Britain, wasn't part of the plan. 'I felt like I was in one of those Coen Brothers' films where the walls start to close in.' He called the Rouxs and was relieved to find them relaxed about the matter.

Gradually things began to pick up. They cashed in on the festive season by opening for Christmas Day and New Year's Eve, resulting in a period when the money just seemed to be tumbling in. 'We took ten grand in a week. So I got the guys in to give us a quote on redoing the kitchen, but then we looked at the figures in the New Year and we'd lost a fortune in that trading period.'

The financial situation remained interesting for some time to come. 'The first couple of years were just a blur ... with the money problems, working to three in the morning and getting up at five thirty. I'm not sure how I managed to come through that mentally and physically.'

Sometimes, I'm told, a bit of hardship is good for you, and I can accept the logic of that. So long as it's somebody else who's learning things the difficult way. There was to be no new kitchen for the time being and he would have to manage with the very limited equipment (including an oven with just one temperature) that he had inherited.

This was, of course, a hindrance, but it was also a riddle asking to be solved, a discipline that required a thorough understanding of what was going on in the cooking processes. Heston Blumenthal likes that kind of thing. 'It was a blessing in disguise because it made me think hard about what was going on and about what sort of food I could produce with these meagre resources.'

There's no question that it helps to have a grand kitchen of generous proportions and all the latest equipment, shiny and straight out of the boxes, but this guarantees nothing other than a big bill. Exactly the same goes for incredibly large kitchen brigades. A good proportion of chefs, if you ask them what they need to improve the quality of their cooking, will have a couple of responses – more (and better) chefs to assist them and, improved (shinier) equipment. Actually, in most cases, what they would be better off doing is thinking a bit more deeply about how they are using the resources they already have. For example, spending time buggering about writing your name on a plate in chocolate is hardly a priority (in fact, I can't think of many more despicable culinary sins – except perhaps baby sweetcorn) and the same goes for a lot of wrapping, rolling, stuffing and sculpting. It's food not Play-Doh. A major part of the skill of a good chef is to make really good food with whatever tools are given to you and that requires intelligent menu planning, a focus on the priorities of good food (which don't include crap art) and good purchasing. And, of course, you also need to learn as you go along.

Which is what Heston Blumenthal was doing, only he'd been doing it for the ten years previously, at home. Much of what he'd done in that time had been trial and error, playing around with ingredients and techniques until, by a process of elimination, he arrived at the result he was after. This was how he came to the chip method, for example, a lot of grit and not much method. 'I'd love to say that I'd got to the point where I was doing that [beginning to use some scientific logic] but I had such dogged determination, I'd take one thing and just flog it to death, doing it like twenty different ways.' Gradually though he had begun to introduce small elements of science into his experiments, things that he'd gleaned from his reading and which started to give direction to his research.

'One of the defining moments was reading Harold McGee's *The Science and Lore of the Kitchen* in 1988 [seven years prior to the Fat Duck]. That whole thing about the browning of meat not actually sealing in the juices like people used to think. That was the spark that made me realise there was another way of looking at this whole thing.' What McGee had worked out was that the traditional way of searing meat at high temperatures to form a crust and thus keep the juices in had, in fact, exactly the opposite effect. He had reached this conclusion by a mixture of chemistry, computer modelling and trial cooking. This was culinary convention overturned, and it excited Blumenthal to think that by adopting a questioning attitude to what was going on in the cooking process you could not only discover what was happening in the pan, you could cook better too. He set to work, on ice creams.

'In terms of breaking down a dish in terms of science, ice cream was the first one ... I came across these tables, formulae for making ice cream. It's all to do with the amount of solids. So if you freeze water it ends up as one big ice block, but if you put some solids in there, it slows down the spread of ice crystals. I found that it's easy to get ice cream that's smooth but it normally has loads of cream and sugar in it. I wanted to get an ice cream that was very clean [tasting] and that melted easily in your mouth, so you didn't have to work it, with no chewiness and fattiness to it. That's why I started having problems because it would crystallise easily because I was going below the threshold of solids. Working on that, all the ice creams we did here at the beginning were all calculated ... and that's where my first foray into more unusual dishes came through ice creams.'

That puzzle, working out how much sugar and cream was needed to stop the ice cream crystallising, made him think about adding other substances instead and savoury things in particular. Though Blumenthal is quick to point out that he isn't the first to go down this route – in the late nineteenth century the remarkable cook Mrs Agnes Bertha Marshall, widely credited with the invention of the ice cream cone, was also a pioneer of innovative ice creams. *Mrs Marshall's Book of Ices* (1885) includes recipes for cucumber, parmesan and curry ice creams.

It was the beginning of the road to what has become the greatest pleasure of Heston Blumenthal's food – the playful way in which he messes about with our preconceptions. I mean, ice cream is going to be sweet, right? Not if it's crab, it isn't. It looks like ice cream and the texture is of ice cream but it tastes of very fresh, straight from the ocean, super-intense crustacean. (Although, according to Blumenthal, if you call it 'crab ice cream' you do taste extra sweetness; call it 'frozen crab parfait' and you don't.) This element of surprise is always with us in the best food, but usually it's about outstripping expectations, coming across food that has an intensity, depth of flavour or degree of precision greater than we've ever experienced before – the lightest pastry, the most delicate pasta. Sometimes it's like that with Blumenthal's cooking too; after all, that's what he's mostly about, trying to work out how to cook familiar things better, like the chips, for example. But then there is this other side to his cooking, the playful side, the impish inclination to play tricks with our senses, and this is where he gets really excited.

When this boyish enthusiasm kicks in and he's toying with the future possibilities of savoury candy floss or candied cauliflower, he resembles Dennis the Menace. He has a look about him that suggests he's about to go out scrumping apples or that he's just devised a ground-breaking way of tormenting the neighbour's cat. In fact, what he's likely to be conjuring up is a way of sealing in an aroma so that, until the flavour bursts in your mouth, you have no inkling of what is on the way; or of adding fermented pipe tobacco to those gorgeous silky chocolates so that after twenty seconds or so of eating one you get a gentle smoky kick at the back of your throat; or of perfecting the sardines on toast sorbet so you not only taste the sardines and the toast but the butter on the toast as well.

It is food that makes you think, but it's not *just* food for thought. I have experienced that elsewhere in Europe, with another chef who is clearly possessed by a spirit of enquiry. I had a meal full of jarring flavours, nine courses of dishes that comprised ingredients never before introduced to each other, of strange textures and weird chemistry. But there was nothing, in any conventional sense, in the way of enjoyment. It seemed to be just an intellectual exercise, food designed to make you think. And it's true, I still think about it now. I think I'm never going within a mile of the place again and I think about the 150 Euros I spent in vain. Blumenthal doesn't do that to you, he's not treating you as if you're some rat on which to try out his culinary experiments. The truth is that he wants to give you food that you'll enjoy and remember. He wants you to like it.

☆☆☆

Plenty of people do. It wasn't long before a few significant reviewers came from the national papers and when the initial verdicts were published they were encouraging. 'I can't remember whether it was Matthew Fort of the *Guardian* or Emily Green of the *Independent* who came and ate first. Later a photographer came to do a picture. I kept a stony face. I was afraid there would be this terrible review, slating us and there I'd be, next to it with a stupid grin on my face.'

As the bookings took off, the financial situation eased and Blumenthal was able to take on some proper assistance in the kitchen and strengthen the front-of-house team. This gave him the chance to develop at an ever quickening pace. When he started out there had been no long-term plan; the aim had been simply to offer good food and stay solvent – 'I had no idea where the restaurant would be in five years' time.' Gradually, the focus of the restaurant became clear; when you came to eat at the Fat Duck the food would distract you, surprise you and sometimes bewilder you. Eating out is entertainment, but this offered an extra dash of theatricality. It was a different sort of spectacle to the classic production that had entranced him as a teenage visitor to Baumanière, but it was drama nevertheless. Dishes would be worked on for months before making it on to the menu, with customers who showed a special interest often finding themselves the recipients of extra works-in-progress. The atmosphere was relaxed, the service correct, informed and breezily enthusiastic. The Fat Duck had developed its own, quite unique mannerisms and like most of the best restaurants they were a clear reflection of the character of the principal actor.

The Fat Duck menu quickly became unrecognisable from the simple French country dishes that Blumenthal had started out with; the cooking reached a level of accomplishment and consistency that put it on a par with the best places to eat in the UK. Alongside the food, a hefty wine list was assembled and it was no real surprise when in January 2000 the Fat Duck received its first Michelin star.

That was the beginning of an incredible sequence without parallel among British chefs. In 2002 the second star followed and then, astonishingly, at the beginning of 2004 the third. Some achievement for a chef who in his entire career spent little more than a month working in anyone else's kitchen, who is otherwise self-taught and who is cooking some of the most daring and therefore risky food in the world. In 2005 *Restaurant Magazine* named The Fat Duck as the best restaurant in the world. The accolades are rewarding but it's apparent that they are not the motivation. The driving forces are instead his insatiable inquisitiveness and his desire to have a restaurant that offers an appropriate setting in which to put his discoveries before the customer. 'I was in the car when the guys rang and told me [about the second star] and it was exciting, but I just thought, right, we're going to need a second sommelier.'

Outside the restaurant he has accrued a network of contacts from various fields but all with the same passion for the science of cooking. He struck up relationships with Peter Barham, a physicist at Bristol University, the Swiss flavouring and fragrance company Firmenich and, eventually, the food scientist Harold McGee, whose book had influenced him so much and whom he greeted with the words 'It's all your fault!' when they met for the first time. He remains as eager as ever to take things forward but it is still a question of balancing time and financial resources. 'It doesn't really get easier. Not in the sense of the time and commitment involved; it's just that the time is spent on more productive things. I have a ten-year-old son, and well, they don't ask to be brought into the world.'

His dreams of a development kitchen where he could spend 'maybe one day a week on it [researching new dishes and techniques], then we'd be rocketing' are now a reality. The thought of having his own laboratory causes him to grin in that Beano way again, remembering a recent expedition to the Firmenich headquarters in Geneva, where they gave him and some of his like-minded cronies a lab for a day. 'There was Harold trying to replace an egg yolk with red wine sauce, me injecting essential essence of bacon into an egg through the shell and Peter experimenting with something else. I just turned to Harold and said, "This is what it's all about isn't it?"'

I asked him if he didn't worry that with all this deconstruction, this forensic approach, he was in danger of taking the magic out of the cooking, losing any sense of wonder. 'No,' he said, 'I don't think so. I'm trying to understand the magic and then use it to do more magic, better magic.'

I've eaten his food, tasted the magic, and it's driven me to believe that maybe there is something in this spirit of enquiry after all. This man is producing some of the most extraordinary and exciting food ever dished up in the UK, and if he ever comes around to my house the first thing I'm going to do is get him in the kitchen cooking chips and making weird ice creams.

And while he's doing that I'm going to slip quietly upstairs and hide my son's fire-red train.

SHAUN HILL

The Quiet Revolutionary

It's ridiculous, I know, but sometimes it can seem like a war.

Why get so passionate about the quality of what we eat in restaurants? Food as a whole is important, clearly, but the really big issues that surround it are elsewhere – why some people simply don't have enough to eat, the control of what goes into our food, the relationship between what we eat and our health. Placed alongside these major concerns the quality of our restaurant food is hardly a priority. Giving it top billing would be like saying that the most important thing about our education system is the quality of the annual school theatrical production. It's an indicator of the vibrancy and health of our food culture and it can feed back in a positive way into the everyday routine of what we eat, but it's hardly among the fundamental issues.

It's an issue nevertheless. There are an estimated 40,000 establishments in the UK alone serving us food at breakfast, lunch, dinner and all points in between. Almost all of them will tell you that it's *good food* they're offering too. Isn't that the most overused and disingenuous quartet of o's? G*oo*d F*oo*d – it even pretends to be a rhyme. How are you supposed to say it, Gewd Fewd or Gud Fud? I have no doubts as to the things I would put into Room 101 and among them would be those stickers and signs with which pubs, restaurants and cafés self-certify the quality of their offering – the ones that say 'Good Food Served Here'. How reassuring is it to see that? Is there really anyone who sees one of those and decides, 'Ah! Good Food Served Here. Well, that's swung it for me, this will be a welcome relief from the mediocrity of the catering on offer elsewhere. In I go!'?

Doesn't it just make you long for an establishment that declares 'Bad Food Served Here (But There's Lots of It And We Won't Charge You Much)'?

I suppose the awkward question is, what constitutes good food anyway? Surely it's just a matter of opinion. Well, yes, much in the same way that it is a matter of opinion that *Rambo 3* is the cinematic superior of *The Godfather* or that Michael Bolton is a greater songwriter than Bob Dylan. You can argue it all you like but if you take *Rambo 3* or Michael Bolton as the title winners in those particular bouts, I'll just have to ask you to step outside and beat you with a set of criteria designed to prove that the latter are better than the former.

In the case of food, here's the armoury, in order of importance.

What makes good food?
1. Good shopping
Without good-quality ingredients there's no good food. Miss this off the list and you have had it. No amount of saucy sexing up will save your liver and bacon.

2. Things cooked accurately
You must be sympathetic to the ingredients, understand what brings out the best in them and be very careful with timings so things are not overcooked or undercooked. Season with thought and care as seasoning is designed to bring out the flavour, not eliminate it.

3. Putting things together that belong together
In food, like much else, there is a host of clichés, classic combinations, ingredients that have become wedded to each other. They have become clichés for a good reason – mostly they work really well together. There are exceptions, every now and then somebody comes up with a slight twist or, in the case of Heston Blumenthal, some explosive device never before conceived of. Those are few and far between; generally the familiar partnerships are the best (with the exception of lamb and redcurrant jelly, of course).

4. Stopping there!
With these three criteria fulfilled we're already at base camp for culinary nirvana. Meet these three demands and the outcome will be some seriously good food. It doesn't seem complicated, does it? And

yet, it's so seldom seen. Even though the standard of eating out in the UK has improved steeply in recent years, it's still far from easy to eat well in many parts of the country and the options for eating badly are myriad. Take the *Good Food Guide* (it's that phrase again) as evidence. It includes about 1,200 restaurants in any annual edition. It would be nice to think that those are at the top of the pyramid, the very best places to eat, and that they're supported by a great mass of really decent places that just can't be squeezed into a paperback book. It's not the case though. The reality is that quite a few of those that are included are not really that great.

So, if it's so simple, why is it that more places don't get it right?

There is a part of the industry that is simply serving up what the market demands: quantity before quality, meat and fish cooked so there's no hint it was ever a living thing, vegetables for which you don't require teeth and food that arrives seconds after you've ordered it. For some customers these are the priorities and it's predictable that a more than adequate supply of places have risen to meet that demand.

There are also heaps of places that aspire to meet a different requirement, that growing element of the market that wants a better experience when eating out. Places where the chefs take themselves seriously and have their names sewn into their whites, where the menus boast of freshly cooked food that you may have to wait for and where the restaurants themselves are described as 'award-winning', 'gastronomic' or 'fine-dining'. Don't rule out the use of the word 'gourmet' either. What is so frustrating and really disappointing is how many of these places, despite their aspirations, also get it so badly wrong. More often than not, the problem is that they've moved on to the next couple of points in our handy criteria for producing good food, without paying proper attention to the first three. They've been distracted by the easy wow of flashy presentation and the mistaken belief that one of the first steps to being a great chef is to have a fertile imagination. As a consequence they end up delivering food that's like Lily Savage on a plate, and it's not funny either.

5. Presentation

In many ways, if proper attention has been paid to 1, 2 and 3, then 5 should look after itself. Food that *is* good tends to look good too. When you see a perfectly cooked piece of fish with bright opal-white flakes, fresh vegetables that look crisp and bright, they send out a signal that they're going to taste as delicious as they appear. And the converse applies – food that looks tired and dull almost certainly is. I don't deny that a bit of care and thought in the way things are arranged on the plate can add to the appeal, but you can't make up for deficiencies elsewhere by making pretty pictures on a dish. Too many restaurant kitchens devote too much of their time to fiddly presentation when their energies would be better spent elsewhere. What they end up with isn't good food, just bad food in fancy dress.

This kind of muddled thinking has gifted us some pointless trends in restaurant food. The compulsion to build towers and other dodgy architecture out of food (the kind of dishes that waiting staff need circus skills to get to the table intact) left me at junior school but for some it persists. As does the fetish for spun sugar cages (like eating cacti), fruit and vegetables carved unconvincingly to resemble wildlife and the need to finish a dish off by putting something on the very top, be it a tiny tomato or a physalis – as if everything has to resemble one of Mr Kipling's cherry Bakewells.

Which brings us to a related and especially virulent bug, the random use of red berries. They get everywhere – strawberries sliced into fantails, redcurrants on the vine, raspberries placed like pert nipples on mounds of just about anything. Nine times out of ten, they're not very good examples of the particular fruit anyway, often out of season and almost always bearing no relation to any of the other ingredients in the dish. Once an oval plate was put in front of me bearing a whole baked trout with the head and tail intact. With the squeamish in mind the eyeball had been scooped from the socket and in the small crater that was left, a raspberry had been thoughtfully placed. At the time it was bewildering and it remains one of the daftest things I have ever been served. Thinking back on it now though, it has come to resemble an inspired piece of comic surrealism. Maybe I was missing something – perhaps I overlooked the René Magritte of the kitchen.

6. Innovation

A lot of chefs like to be different, to come up with new and exciting dishes, and they argue that they need to do this to get noticed, to stand out from the crowd. That kind of argument presumes that there is a wealth of restaurants out there already doing the more familiar kinds of dishes as well as they can be done. There isn't. A really innovative approach for many restaurants and chefs would be to try producing really good classic dishes, consistently well. Before you start attempting to conjure up something new you have to master the basic repertoire. 'He's like Picasso on a plate,' a restaurant owner told me of his chef not so long ago. I've seen Picasso's early stuff, he could really draw. He understood what the fundamentals were, he mastered them and that gave him the capacity to start doing things differently; he had to earn the right to innovate. Cook me a proper steak béarnaise, then we'll talk about Picasso.

The bewildering part is that none of the above is new, revelatory or even remotely contentious. At the turn of the twentieth century the legendary Auguste Escoffier was saying '*fait simple*'. It was also the lifeblood of the hugely influential writings of Elizabeth David and Jane Grigson. Arguably it's a message that has rarely been trumpeted as loudly as in recent years – through the cooking and restaurants of Marco Pierre White in the late nineties, and the cuisine and media work of Gary Rhodes, Rick Stein and others.

But whenever I need to give an example of a current working chef who more than any other represents the triumph and potential of (deceptively) simple food, I have no hesitation in always turning to the same place, Ludlow in Shropshire.

☆☆☆

Think of Ludlow and, if you have more than a passing interest in food, it's hard not to think of Shaun Hill. Of course, he's not the only culinary star in this remarkably blessed Shropshire town, but you get the feeling that, if you took his Merchant House restaurant away, the bonds holding this cluster of great cooking together would be that much looser.

And yet, the operation that has had such a magnetic effect is of Lilliputian proportions. It's a half-timbered Jacobean house on the edge of the town, at the foot of the hill where Ludlow rolls steeply away from its central highpoint back down towards the River Teme. You don't have to crouch to get in, but the medieval proportions of the building seem hardly tall enough to sustain its two storeys. It's a diminutive restaurant with just twenty-two seats and no need for a personnel department. Besides the chef, there is his wife, Anja, and a waiter, and as a consequence you can never be quite sure which Shaun Hill you're going to encounter. Right now, he's in receptionist mode and, typically, his technique for dealing with enquiries can best be described as individual.

'Yes, we are open that night and we do have a table available,' he says, in response to a phone enquiry about New Year's Eve. It soon becomes clear that the caller is hoping that there will be some extra pomp incorporated into the evening's proceedings – perhaps a piper or a troupe of acrobats. 'No, we won't be doing anything like that,' Hill says. 'We're a small restaurant and we'll just be offering our usual sort of menu.' Then he adds, drily, 'But the good news is that we won't be charging anything extra, either.'

This incident goes a long way to encapsulating Hill's approach to running his restaurant. It's readily apparent that he has a very clear idea of what the Merchant House is about, and there is no chance of him falling into the trap of trying to be all things to all men. With his unruly grey-flecked hair, owlish glasses and effortless wit there is a little of the detached, academic air about him and he could be mistaken for an impish, but brilliant university professor, but it would be a mistake to underestimate his focus and very singular approach to the business of running a restaurant. After all, he is in possession (according to *Restaurant Magazine* in 2003) of the fourteenth best restaurant in the world, a Michelin star, 8/10 in the *Good Food Guide* and most importantly a full reservations book for months ahead.

☆☆☆

A conversation with Shaun Hill can bring you almost as much pleasure as his food and he too seems happy to talk. Perhaps his easy eloquence stems from the atmosphere in the London home of his youth in the fifties, where his father, a journalist 'who knew all sorts of people, especially in the literary world', regularly invited distinguished guests for dinner. On these occasions he would bring home goodies procured from delicatessens such as Schmidts in Charlotte Street or

Del Monico's in Old Compton Street, where you could buy what were at that time quite exotic things such as peppers and olive oil. The trouble was his father had no idea how to cook them and his mother's kitchen skills were no more than adequate. 'One time he bought a load of eels. My mother's family come from Lough Neagh where eels are what you eat, but she had been brought up in Connecticut and would no more know how to cook an eel than fly to the moon. In the end he took them to the pub and got them severely drunk (the guests not the eels) while she did what she could with the bloody things and then they came back and ate them and everything was good. A valuable lesson in the power of aperitifs in a dodgy meal.'

The staple diet of the household was not nearly so adventurous. This was before the onslaught of convenience foods and Hill remembers 'a lot of sausages' being on the menu, and while he developed a typical teenager's enthusiasm for eating, he won't pretend that he showed any early signs of an inclination to cook. 'It's easy to read things back into the past which weren't significant at the time. I can do that, and my mother was even worse. As I started cooking, she started remembering that I was *always* interested in it, but *I* remember being interested in climbing fences and staying out late at night and those sort of things.'

One is hesitant then, as a third party, to start reading too much significance, food-wise, into any of his early history; I might just be imagining it. It does appear, though, that his father, if not exactly a bon viveur, had at least an above average interest in food and that his son, as a result, got to sniff the aroma of the world of eating out at an early age. 'He enjoyed eating. He ate out periodically, it wasn't a thing that he did a lot, but from time to time, which was more than most people did. I remember my first proper meal out with him which I paid for – he liked other people to pay – it was at a very good Polish restaurant in Hampstead called Cresta and I had sort of stuffed braised rump steak or something and he had sweetbreads to start and I thought, 'funny things to eat', but it was interesting and most of my enjoyment has come this way, worked from the grub backwards rather than from the skills forwards.'

Before the youngster had the resources to treat his dad, he and his siblings would be taken out themselves to less notable destinations such as Lyon's Corner House in Marble Arch 'where a waiter in tails would serve you something like chicken in a basket'. He remembers the emergence in the mid-fifties of the first Indian restaurant that opened in Camden Town market. "It had a domestic stove and a man that cooked one type of curry, I think he eventually moved up to two types of curry and you could have a soft drink with it and read the *Christian Science Monitor*. That was five shillings.'

Hill appears to have been mildly charmed by these outings and took some enjoyment in the theatre that went on around him as he ate, but it would be wrong to suggest that these were the sparks that lit some latent bonfire within him.

☆ ☆ ☆

Hill began work at the Baltic State Steamship Line in the ticketing department where he had responsibility for looking after the English-speaking passengers. He readily confesses that he wasn't at all good at the job and it was little surprise to him when he was sacked. A stint with Thomas Cook as a travel adviser followed before he was offered a relatively lucrative job in local government and took it.

I probably ought to be a little sensitive here. I used to work in local government too and some of the people I left behind there are still friends, but I can't help but report that my experience, almost three decades later, wasn't so far removed from his recollection. 'It was desperate, full of people drinking strong tea out of the same mug at the same time every day … it was pre-computer and everything was in huge folders and as I looked at the endless racks of them I could just see a horrific career stretching in front of me, with the prospect of turning into these people.'

When he said this to me, I could see those aisles of cardboard files too – eight-foot-high narrow corridors in the dusty confines of Cardiff City Council Planning and Development Department, Development Control Division. Development Control is where they say yeah or nay to your planning application. Before too long you find that the greatest pleasures to be had from the job are being as rude to the applicants as they are to you and making sure you get the better of the flexitime system. My immediate boss on the fifth floor was a mentor in this respect. The flexitime machine was on the ground floor adjacent to the lift door, which meant he could take the lift down, leave his briefcase in the lift, clock out and step back into the lift to continue to the basement car park. A perfect routine which he followed each day without fail, until one afternoon the lift door closed unexpectedly with the case still inside and sped back up to the fifth floor. He was stranded, waiting for the lift to return so he could reclaim his case. The thought that all this was now occurring on his own time was too much for him and he began to kick the lift door wildly before head-butting it Yosser Hughes-style. It was a disturbing tragicomic episode and, like Shaun Hill, I knew then that I had to get out.

By this point he had begun to cook at home, mainly inspired by Anja, his Finnish wife, whom he had met while working at the shipping line, but he was still more interested in eating food than making it. 'Anja was a good cook, she made good things. I'd never had proper salad dressings before or even a properly made home-made salad cream.'

Having decided that he definitely didn't want a career as a public servant he was left to ponder his options. The interest in food had developed and although he was far from obsessed with the subject, the connection he had established was enough to make him at least entertain a future as a chef. The trigger came when a local restaurant in Southgate advertised in the *Evening Standard* for a commis chef at the rate of £11 per week; he was currently earning £18. He went along for the interview and explained himself to the very traditional Austrian chef as best he could. He was listened to politely and sent on his way. 'It was "Don't call us, we'll call you," but in those days nobody wanted to be a cook and the only other person who turned up for the interview didn't show up for the job. So I got a telegram, because I wasn't on the phone, saying there was an opportunity for me at the Cherry Tree.'

He managed to sub enough money for a couple of uniforms and on the following Monday he turned up there instead of going to work at his usual place. He was contracted to do five and a half days, but worked the other one and a half too for the sake of an extra £2 10s. 'It meant serious poverty but it was what I wanted to do, or rather I didn't really know I wanted to do it at the time but I thought it *might* be what I wanted to do. Straight away I started to enjoy the swagger of the kitchen and you got to eat very well even if you couldn't pay the bills very well.'

The kitchen was run along very traditional lines, with nine chefs. 'At that point, you got the odds and ends of Europe there, anybody with work permit difficulties or psychiatric or alcohol problems would be sort of compressed into this and in that way it was quite fascinating.'

The long hours and rugged atmosphere of the kitchen came as something of a shock to the twenty-year-old. He went in at eight to cook the staff breakfast and finished that shift at two thirty, but he'd reappear at four thirty and stay to the finish at about eleven thirty. His £11 was a weekly wage, whatever the hours, and when you consider that his rent at the time was £6 it's apparent that the financial rewards were limited in the extreme.

Nevertheless, he quickly grew to relish the robust exchanges brought on by the mutual loathing between the chefs, the waiting staff and the management. In the kitchen itself there was a rough rivalry between the sections and little time for niceties. 'No one had ever been that rude to me before. A Polish man was the sauce cook and I was his commis and he moved between gentle and charming to hysteria with a phenomenal grasp of bad language. He would also be always trying to avoid work. I mean it's a lunatic job anyway because it's such hard work and lousy hours, to avoid the little bits that make the difference strikes me as being meaningless. So he'd make hollandaise in the evening and, of course, you weren't meant to retain anything that doesn't keep or might poison someone, so he would hide it until the next day and try and bring it back with béchamel.'

In many ways the food quickly became the least enlightening aspect of the job. In time-honoured fashion, gravy browning was liberally applied to almost everything of a suitable hue, the tomato soup, though home-made, was inferior to Heinz, and the same went for the minestrone. He was, however, learning a lot about the mechanics of the kitchen operation – how a menu and its individual dishes can be broken down into separate jobs and then brought back together at service. 'You get to understand how some people could make a whole career in a kitchen but couldn't cook you a three-course meal because they've always washed the spinach or grilled things but they have never, ever made a sponge. It's odd in that you never get the whole experience.'

He found the rigour of the job to be satisfying, and with the exception of the money he felt that things had fallen into place. There was by then a certainty that he would make a career as a chef. He also realised that he didn't just want to spend his working life confined in the limited routines of the traditional kitchen, but wanted to develop and learn.

Robert Carrier had opened a restaurant in Islington.

A job was advertised in the press; it was once again for a commis chef. For Shaun Hill, having worked his way an increment or two up the salary scale at the Cherry Tree, this was going to mean another career move that resulted in less income than he was leaving behind. (Continue this way and after another couple of changes of restaurant, *he* would be paying *them*.) The reduction in income would be a difficult pill to swallow but, as we have seen elsewhere in this book, it's not an uncommon medicine. Carrier's was an exciting opportunity, almost without compare in London; in the mid-sixties only Le Gavroche could be said to have the same magnetism for a chef. He went for the job and got it. It would prove an excellent decision. 'That's where I really started to enjoy it and it [a career as a chef] went from being a vague interest to something much more consuming.'

Carrier was already known for his writing in *The Times* (which Shaun Hill had read and liked) and his bestselling 1963 book *Great Dishes of the World*. The title was no idle boast. Carrier had indeed eaten all over the world and, while he wasn't at the stove, he knew how things should taste. 'Although we didn't think it at the time we [the chefs] owed a lot to Carrier. He didn't cook, but he'd been everywhere, he'd lived in the South of France, he was passionate about ingredients and he insisted things tasted right. There was stuff there I'd never seen before, I'd never seen radiccio or trevise. We learned how to do more interesting things with artichokes and other vegetables, a lot of the Provençal types of dishes. He also liked to have at least one or two dishes on the menu that weren't French.'

It was a lavish style, highly charged with butter, cream and cheese, and Hill himself describes some of the food as 'super dinner-party dishes' but that didn't make them any less interesting. As with so many things, it ain't what you do, it's the way that you do it. Take the humble quiche, for example … 'The quiches they made at Carrier's were brilliant; the pastry cook made very, very good, very thin, crisp short pastry. We only ever cooked them off in batches, and they were made just with double cream. You'd die of cholesterol now if you had two. I knew them well because we never reheated them, when they were cold we cooked another batch. So my family lived on whatever the quiche on the menu was for years … It's taken us a long time to face them again, but properly made they were a delight.'

Quiche is not a term often seen on restaurant menus these days, partly out of embarrassment I suspect. It's one of those dishes that has become a cliché and suffered from being seized on by commercial companies and less caring kitchens which for reasons of finance and convenience, cut corners. Once dishes have been through this process, their supermarket manifestation eventually takes over in the public mind, they become a travesty of their former selves and it is then very difficult to serve them again. In recent years there has been a trend towards reclaiming some of these dishes, and taking them back to their former incarnations – in other words, doing them properly. A tournedos Rossini made with foie gras and truffles can still be a thing of joy, banishing memories of the much more common Ardennes pâté and soggy crouton version. Marco Pierre White became especially good at this in the late nineties with dishes such as 'roast chicken, properly garnished'. Sunday lunch effectively, but done, as it says in the title, *properly*. And that, of course, is always the important thing.

Whatever the style of the cooking, the point is that Carrier's was real, authentic and honest. This was a world away from the 'mock grandeur of faked-up haute cuisine' that he'd been used to, where a dumbed-down version of *le répertoire de la cuisine* prevailed, margarine often took the place of butter and if a short-cut was available, it was gratefully taken. At Carrier's there was real care, it was 'somewhere that took real pleasure in the business of eating'.

This view of Robert Carrier's worth and contribution is refreshing, because his extravagant style, both on the plate and in his demeanour, was not universally popular at the time and suffered something of a backlash when cleaner, less creamy and alcoholic styles of cooking later became fashionable. 'Elizabeth David was big at the time and I'd read all her books and she despised Robert Carrier, she thought he was like a circus clown ... partly, of course, that was because he opened a cookware shop next to hers and that went down very badly indeed.'

Carrier's allowed Shaun Hill to quickly accrue a wider range of kitchen experiences. He took on the pastry when the pastry chef was away and he was eventually promoted to take charge of what he calls the 'super-larder' section. The larder in a restaurant kitchen is the area responsible for the preparation of foods to be served cold and in the case of Carrier's this meant a lot of time spent making terrines, which were phenomenally popular at that time. Carrier had also opened a new restaurant at Hintlesham Hall in Suffolk and his Islington restaurant became responsible for supplying it with terrines as well. In addition, Hill was often charged with responsibility for feeding the staff. He seems to have had something of a fetish for this in his early career because it offered him the opportunity to depart from the more repetitive elements of the job and it was the one chance he got to cook a whole meal.

'The standard of the staff meal is appalling at some very good places and I find that to be quite strange. Although it needn't be anything complicated or expensive, there's no reason why it shouldn't be good and interesting ... and also it offers a valuable learning experience for somebody junior ... I'd regularly make the meal for all of the cooks, although a chap called Bernard did the waiters. He'd make them meatballs every second day – which they despised. The more they despised it the more triumphantly he served them up – Good man, I still keep in touch with him.'

He was enjoying himself. Carrier's kitchen offered him a liberty and variety that would have been absent in most London kitchens. He was also getting to work with good fresh ingredients, many of them unfamiliar. The lack of regard for convention in Carrier's was to play a large part in shaping what has been a notably non-conformist career, but at the time it was something of a risk to be outside the mainstream of the profession.

'I knew from other people in the trade that this was a quite disastrous set of career moves that I was making. I mean I worked in quite maverick places whereas I should have been at the Savoy or the Dorchester and then into one of those large hotels that, say, Grand Metropolitan or Fortes would be running which did imitations of their food. But I couldn't bring myself to care about that. So in that respect, I've never plotted a course.'

After four years, with family commitments to consider, he left Carrier's in search of advancement and a better wage, re-emerging in Soho at one of Britain's best-known restaurants (though largely for things other than the food), the Gay Hussar.

☆ ☆ ☆

In October 2003 it was reported that a cabal of Britain's top union leaders met to plan a revolt against Tony Blair and the Labour government. Their chosen vehicle was a conference debate on foundation hospitals. Sure enough, on the Wednesday of the Labour Party conference, the platform was defeated and the 'awkward squad', as they had been dubbed, succeeded in giving the government a bloody nose.

According to the reports they hatched their plot over dinner. Not an unusual occurrence in the world of politics, but whereas Messrs Brown and Blair had hammered out their leadership pact in the of-the-minute cool nineties environment of Granita in Islington, the union leaders met in the profoundly Old Labour haunt of the Gay Hussar in Soho. (Unreconstructed Old Labourites searching for straws to clutch at might take comfort from the fact that Granita closed its doors for the final time in 2003, the same year that the Gay Hussar celebrated fifty years in business.)

An early supporter of the Greek Street Hungarian restaurant was Aneurin Bevan, and it seems to have been his devotion to the place that fired its popularity with the left, which has endured to the present day. Michael Foot held his ninetieth birthday celebrations there in 2003. You don't keep a restaurant going by appealing exclusively to the left wing of the Labour Party though, especially these days (Shaun Hill's twenty-four seats would probably accommodate that) and the restaurant has survived on a history of gossip and intrigue almost as rich as the Hungarian-style food.

The Gay Hussar is synonymous with the name of the late Victor Sassie, the man who ran it during its heyday. Following the war, Sassie was employed in the Budapest restaurant in Dean Street and he encouraged the belief that he was of Hungarian origin. In reality he was from Barrow-in-Furness, the son of Italian immigrants, but there was no shortage of genuine Eastern European blood in the place. 'The Gay Hussar was an interesting throwback. It was largely Austrians and Hungarians, most of whom had fought on the wrong side during the last war and those who hadn't had come over in 1956 [as a result of the uprising] and at least one of them wasn't allowed back into Hungary because he'd shot the sergeant and nipped over the border and that was obviously against the law ... even after tempers had cooled. The kitchen was full of the most right-wing fascists you could ever wish to meet. One had been on the Russian front with Hitler's armies for six years, the rest had escaped from Hungary ... One year Frank Cousins who had been head of the TUC [and was to become a minister in Harold Wilson's cabinet] came down and gave us all two hundred fags and I thought if you knew these people you wouldn't be giving them those. I smoked at the time, and I smoked like a chimney in the kitchen by the way all the way through ... I don't think we ever poisoned anybody.'

There was no particular structure in the kitchen and an absence of any meaningful titles. 'The head chef wasn't really a head chef, he worked straight shifts and came in with a briefcase and called himself a kitchen manager ... a lovely old Hungarian guy whom Victor had known for years. He'd done Victor Sassie favours when he was on his uppers.'

Whatever his position, Hill was being paid better than he ever had been before. The money side of life was further helped by the fact that he also did the books which gave him unique access to Sassie's office and the curiosities contained therein. 'I went to the office on a Friday morning to do that instead of cooking and he could hear everything because there were just baby alarms or listening devices if you want it to sound more sinister, on every floor. So he could hear what was happening, including in the kitchen ... so he could hear them saying what a bastard he was.'

It was an insight that much more recently enabled him to solve a mystery for former Labour cabinet minister Roy, now Lord, Hattersley when he visited the Merchant House. Hattersley recalled an occasion when he had gone to the Gay Hussar with then Prime Minister Jim Callaghan to discuss whether to call an election. As they departed Victor Sassie said to them, 'I think you've come to the right decision.'

'How did he know that?' Hattersley had enquired of the chef.

'Well, *I know* how he knew that,' Hill was able to reply. 'Because he'll have heard every word!'

Shaun Hill clearly relished the excitement and intrigue of the place. Out front were the most powerful politicians of the day deciding the fate of the country over dishes of wild cherry soup, or sharing gossip with journalists as they dined on stuffed cabbage and smoked goose, while in the kitchen a rugged ragbag of chefs schemed and plotted

– procuring wine from the off-licence next door by way of a pulley system that allowed them to send up some goulash every day in the certain knowledge of a bottle of wine coming down in return.

On top of all that, the pay and conditions easily outstripped anything he had experienced, particularly in respect of the one benefit so close to his heart. 'You were allowed to eat whatever you wanted and if you didn't have time to make it, Victor would come and cook it for you. If you wanted a Wiener schnitzel or whatever, that was fine, there were no restrictions on what you could have. I *really enjoyed* that.' (You need to hear the way he says 'really enjoyed' to appreciate the depth of his relish.)

Victor Sassie's benevolence extended to the staff's pay packets but there was payback too. 'Victor paid everybody more than they were worth, including me, and was astonishingly rude to you. If you broke anything, you replaced it. I made a salad wrong once and he translated it as "Shaun's mistake" in Hungarian and it was sold as my mistake on the menu. But underneath his very gruff exterior he was a good-natured man.'

And he ran a worthwhile restaurant too. Hill became a fan of the middle-European cooking that was served up. Again, he was working with the best ingredients available, sticking to fresh vegetables rather than easier, cheaper and massively inferior tinned or frozen versions that were still commonly used elsewhere. 'I loved the food, it was exciting. I've been back to Budapest ever since. I have a Hungarian dessert, probably the only thing I can still remember how to make. I went back to Budapest and all of a sudden it was enjoying a huge revival. It's called Somloi [pronounced *shomloy*] and it was like a sort of trifle … the flavouring was crushed walnuts, apricot jam and rum with chocolate on the top … [in Budapest] a light bulb went on and I thought, I used to make that, so I put it on the menu. I have a warm feeling towards that food.'

Hill progressed quickly through the ranks at that stage of his career. His explanation for this is simply that the competition wasn't up to much. A little too modest perhaps, but it's interesting to hear him say this, particularly when he makes comparisons with the situation today. 'I progressed quickly because it wasn't difficult. It's much more difficult for people now because there is much more competition, much brighter people coming into the trade … much more motivated. There were still a lot of people there because they couldn't do much else or couldn't think of much else. It would still have been a very odd person who spent any of his wages on eating out.'

Catering as a last resort, full of people there as a final or only option. People with no real passion for food, who just did their required hours, picked up a pay packet and got on with doing the things that really interested them – this all sounds very familiar and it doesn't have the ring of yesterday's news. Every year it's the subject of debate at conferences, seminars and wherever chefs gather to discuss the problems of the industry. Finding people who want to be in a kitchen as much for the love of it as for the remuneration is no easy task. Put an advert out for a chef and see how many get back to you with a first question of 'What are the hours and what's the pay?' It will be the majority. What you want to hear is what sort of thing will I be cooking? Who will I be working with? What will I learn?

Shaun Hill's recollection of the situation a few decades back adds an interesting perspective. It's easy to forget that despite the difficulties, the situation has improved significantly. At that time there were few role models in the profession, today we are inundated by chefs that by one route or another have made a name for themselves. It no longer looks like a dead-end career and, while there are still plenty of kitchens populated by those who could find nowhere else to go, they are in the company of a healthy swathe of individuals with real ambition as chefs. The trouble is ambition is not enough on its own. Kitchens may not be quite the workhouses that they once were but you still don't get anywhere significant without putting yourself through some real pain. Whatever your view on the rights and wrongs of this (and I've personally had a lifelong nervousness about anything described as 'character building'), it's still the reality of the job today.

Hill made his way around the kitchen, picking up the craft skills that enabled him to move on. Learning the basic preparations, how to bone and fillet things, were the skills that he had to acquire and, once he had them, he found it relatively easy to move through the ranks. It wasn't, however, part of any great scheme to get to the top. 'I don't think there has ever been a long-term plan – apart from being rich and famous and that's still on the back burner. The problem with thinking too far ahead is it stops your concentration on what you're doing. So how I work is I do it while I really enjoy it and when I stop enjoying it I decide it's time to go. This very regularly seems like a dumb move at the time. But in order to do anything well you have to be completely, maybe not obsessed, but committed, not looking to the next chance. The next thing comes at that point.'

Hill wasn't sure that he could continue on this unconventional path. He hadn't yet seen the inside of a high-powered traditional kitchen and there was the niggling thought that there was an embarrassing gap in his experience. And anyway, after the circus of the Gay Hussar it was understandable that he felt 'like going for a more structured job. You get pangs where you feel you ought to be doing something sensible.'

Sometimes you have to go there to come back. Joining the Intercontinental Hotel on Hyde Park Corner wasn't quite like walking into the Dorchester or the Savoy, chiefly because whereas they were steeped in history and tradition, the Intercontinental was just about to open. It was, however, a huge operation with ninety chefs and a classic organisational structure – the hotel's fine-dining restaurant was to be called Le Soufflé. '[Peter] Kromberg, who was the chef there, was a master craftsman and an organisation man. He was very good, he commanded respect without dread, I never heard him raise his voice.'

Hill may have made the decision to go straight for a while, but it was apparent to Kromberg that in order to get the best out of his new charge, he would need to bend the rules somewhat. 'It was quite obvious that I was not going to fit into a kitchen with ninety chefs and a huge roster. So he did my roster personally, and I got to cook things. We had a restaurant where we souffléd everything and I souffléd enough for a lifetime there.'

Initially the job was stimulating. The months leading up to the opening were heady with anticipation and there was the rare treat of having the time to actually work on dishes and recipes in preparation for the new restaurant. There was also the fascination of witnessing the organisation of such a vast catering machine at work. These were learning experiences but there was a bigger lesson behind them. 'Most of all it was important for me that I found out it wasn't what I wanted to do. That I didn't want to go to meetings, to move away from the stove, that what I enjoyed doing was the physical hands-on cooking. I like talking about cooking, I even like writing about cooking, but I don't like having meetings about profit margins and friction between departments – "housekeeping think the kitchen are using too many rags to wipe down with" – well, I couldn't give a bugger about that. I'm not interested in scoring points, I'm not even interested in what title I hold in the great scheme of things.'

For the first time, however, he was among people who *did* have an eye for their progression. The staff who had been recruited to the Intercontinental in the mid-seventies were attracted by the promise of an ambitious and bold new venture. As a result, they were characterised by greater drive than Hill had been used to and a greater clarity of purpose as far as their careers were concerned. 'Japanese, a lot more French boys and Germans and Swiss. Very, very motivated, very ambitious. It was much more like you might experience now in say a Gordon Ramsay-type kitchen, where people have got their eye on specific goals, they've got a list of people that they'll have to work with. [For instance] the sauce cook took a plane on his day off and turned up at [Paul] Bocuse's restaurant, asked for a job with no money, got a weekend job, got himself another job in Lyon [for the rest of the week]. Came back and gave his notice in. Because that was where he wanted to go to.'

He'd dipped his finger in and decided it wasn't to his taste. If that was the big lesson that he left the Intercontinental with, there was a smaller but still significant message accompanying it.

It was a key time in discovering what he wanted to do with food. He was enrolled on a course in chocolate-making and sugar-pulling, things that were an essential part of the way the hotel wanted to present its food. It's worth noting that this was a kitchen that employed a couple of people just to do ice-carving. 'It was interesting to learn how to do it, [but] again the light bulb goes on, what for? This is a diversion from the main thing which is the food ought to taste nice. After that it should be interesting or look good, but after that. It's knowing how to do things and then deciding not to do them. It's easy to get caught up in the trade with things that bring you kudos with your peers and those tend to be craft things rather than flavour. I mean you have to have knife skills in order to get through the work in time and you have to understand how the muscles on a calf operate and which are good for what. You can't just move in and play with it, you have to understand that.'

It was an approach that was beginning to get some wind behind it. Potent writing on the country cooking of France, Italy and Spain, most influentially by Elizabeth David from the mid-fifties on, stirred an interest in reproducing the regional cooking of those countries. 'I was enthused by Elizabeth David ... she made you feel like eating the food and she removed food completely from that strange straitjacket of false grandeur that it had got itself into. It became accessible and ... worthy of conversation. The sort of peasant cooking that she did in the French book especially made you feel like eating cassoulet.

These things didn't require an unlimited budget, just access to the raw materials.'

The raw materials were appearing. Better and more interesting fresh produce started to become more readily available and not just at a few specialist shops and this, partly at least, was due to the eulogising of Elizabeth David and the like. It was an earlier and more generalised version of the Delia effect, demand creating supply.

'Similarly, technology changed and things which were amazingly labour-intensive became very easy. The food processor and blenders took away an awful lot of the work that went into sieving mixes for a mousse and all that sort of thing, not just for the restaurants but for the home cook too. And the more demanding people became, the better it was for us cooks.'

Or perhaps more accurately, for those cooks who were interested in producing really good food. As we've seen, the customer is not always the friend of good food. Restaurants exist to meet demand and if the customer has no desire to eat a proper bouillabaisse, daube of beef or choucroute then there's not a whole lot of point in offering them, however much the chef might want to cook them. So, the more familiar these kinds of dishes became to the public the more they wanted to eat them in restaurants, which was good news for chefs of Mr Hill's ilk.

As was nouvelle cuisine. I sense dangerous territory here: although the term is thirty years old, it's still common enough currency in conversation and it's rarely used as flattery. That's because of what it has come to represent in many people's minds – small amounts of food for big amounts of money. This, as Karl Marx might say, was not the original intention. In fact, the values behind nouvelle cuisine were pretty much in line with the ones Shaun Hill is describing – that it was about time restaurants stopped covering up badly cooked food with ultra-rich sauces and theatrical garnishes and got down to serving up dishes that tasted of their main ingredients and looked good for the simple reason that they were good. More honesty on the plate, in other words.

There was some heavy philosophising behind the movement which originated with the critics Gault and Millau and there was even a poster campaign to support it. It's sobering to recognise too, that as early as the beginning of the seventies part of the impetus was the recognition of the effects of food on health, and spun into the nouvelle cuisine movement was an intention to encourage the use of less fatty foods and reduce the amount of processed food in the diet. Great innovations can be like Chinese whispers though, people take the most obvious parts and strip them out until you're left with nothing but a cartoon version of the original. When nouvelle cuisine was at its height, it was indeed about morsels of food cut into pretty shapes and arranged on unfeasibly large plates. And there's nothing clever about that.

Shaun Hill is evidence that the straightforward roots on which this new style was founded were quite different from the pretentious fruit it gave birth to. He is not a chef whose food could be described as ungenerous in any sense, yet, when asked for his greatest influences he cites the emergence of nouvelle cuisine and one of its main architects, Paul Bocuse of Lyon. 'When nouvelle cuisine really arrived with Bocuse's famous meal for Valéry Giscard d'Estaing [Bocuse had been awarded the Legion of Honour by the President and created "La Soupe aux Truffes V.G.E." for the occasion] I must say I took my hat off to that ... and I looked to that new French cooking, for how the food would be.'

British chefs had largely taken their lead from France and in particular the grander style of French cooking. Now Hill was also looking further afield, to Italy. 'Instead of Italian food being a ghastly trattoria menu of chicken cacciatore and a few other horrible faked up things, suddenly people realised [there was] all that great domestic cooking ... because it's basically a domestic cuisine, the same as Indian is. It all suddenly started to blossom, so you'd have had to have had no palate not to get really interested by it or enthused by those developments.'

☆ ☆ ☆

It didn't take long for it to become clear to Hill that his original instincts had been correct and cooking in a vast operation like the Intercontinental Hotel was not for him.

David Levin, an hotelier who had worked his way up from the basement of the industry, had launched the Capital Hotel in Knightsbridge in 1971. It started out with just ten rooms and a restaurant, but after a shaky start, garnered a formidable reputation and an enthusiastic following. Five years on, the restaurant had gained a Michelin star but was going through an uncertain period, and David Levin was looking for a new chef. He invited Hill to tea.

'They'd been through a difficult time because Richard Shepherd [now owner of Langan's Brasserie] had left after a disagreement over the Greenhouse [Levin's Mayfair restaurant] taking all the recipes with him ... It had a great reputation for food and I'd eaten very well there, so I was flattered [to be approached].' Hill was offered the job of working head chef. He would be overseen by Brian Turner whose partnership with Richard Shepherd had brought the star to the hotel.

Working head chef is the kind of title that raises all sorts of questions – such as, isn't the adjective superfluous? Surely the job description of any head chef requires that they work? Well, a useful comparison is in football where you nowadays often have somebody called the coach or the team manager but above them you have a director of football. It's the coach, or in this case the working head chef, who gets their hands dirty while the director of football, or the executive chef, sets the overall direction for the club, or the kitchen.

This has been going on for years, although there has been something of an explosion in these titles recently. The title of executive chef, or similar, can be very useful when well-known chefs either lose the inclination or don't have the time to do much actual cooking. It also means that they can spread themselves across several restaurants, all of which benefit from the association with their name. There are various degrees of this, ranging from a total departure from the stove to those who take the title but still remain very hands-on in the kitchen, but broadly it means you have someone under you who takes charge of the day-to-day running of the kitchen – the *working* head chef in other words. As we've seen, Shaun Hill wouldn't have wanted it any other way and the Capital, because of the unusual geography of its kitchen set-up, demanded more cooking from a head chef than most restaurants.

'What was good about it was that the head chef or the sous chef cooked every meal. Because of the physical structure of the place it didn't work in the conventional way. It had been designed to be a steak bar, so there was a cutaway little kitchen in the restaurant with just room for a chef and a commis ... all the prep was done by a series of cooks, mostly young lads, in a room upstairs and then you went down to this service and cooked everything. You had an intercom and you'd say [imitates barking into the intercom] more fresh bread-crumbs, more chopped shallots, cut a few more racks of lamb. In a way it was ideal, drudgery was done by other people ... and you actually got to cook everything. You could see the people that were eating it and they could see you and so you had to be careful that everything was spot on.'

Having worked in some very varied venues and made his way up through the ranks, Hill was much more confident of his own abilities and was quite clear about the style of cooking he preferred. Although the mechanics of the Capital meant that he got to cook a lot of the food himself, his influence on the restaurant was heavily constrained. '... a kitchen with two head chefs is about as good an idea as having two mothers-in-law or two wives ... it's not a great system. The second thing was you couldn't change anything on the menu.'

The latter problem, it seems, was down to the trepidation that a Michelin star can install. Chefs and restaurateurs can become like rabbits caught in headlights, transfixed by the glow of the fabled star and afraid to move, just in case the beam doesn't follow them and their time in the starlight is over. And because Michelin don't tell you why you've got the star, it's impossible to know what might lose you it – the removal of a dish from the menu, a change in crockery, the colour of the curtains. A state of near paralysis can ensue and it can get pretty silly.

'I wanted to change a duck dish ... I wanted to put one of Elizabeth David's on. It was wrapped and poached, it was lovely, like a warm version of Lady Llanover's salt duck. Then the sauce was made with the liver and some of the cooking juices ... I thought it would be a brilliant dish, but there was no way. The menu had been put in [about five years before] by a man called Pierre Gleize of a restaurant called La Bonne Etape, in France ... They used at that time Anchor butter ... because that's what they'd used when they opened, they'd got a Michelin star and they weren't changing anything ... you didn't tamper with success. If a food guide came out and it mentioned a dish and that dish had been due to be chopped or reshuffled, it would have to come back.'

You get the sense that the place took itself rather too seriously for Shaun Hill's liking and while he appreciated the commitment to high standards and the attention to detail, there was a tendency to Kafkaesque bureaucracy that irked him. 'We had Michel Roux and Len Evans [the Australian winemaker] coming for a special meal. One of the specialities was a scallop terrine ... with sea urchins. Now when they opened or when Pierre Gleize put this menu in, they couldn't get sea urchins, so [despite the title of the dish] they just left them out. Now the point came when Michel Roux was coming to dinner and *he'd* be able to tell ... So we had this meeting ... with the head waiter, the restaurant manager, Turner, myself and David Levin, to discuss whether to make a batch with sea urchins or to take it off the menu ... It was just such a joke, and the poor old restaurant manager, nobody had ever told him and he'd been telling people that the red bit which was the coral [from the scallops] in the middle, like a Japanese flag, had sea urchins in it. There was something slightly farcical about it ...'

☆☆☆

Shaun Hill is a thoughtful man – I've always done a lot of thinking too, but after forty years, I've yet to reach any conclusions. The noticeable thing about Shaun Hill is that you get the powerful impression that he has established a pretty clear idea of what he's about and he is

evidently very focused. Yet it's not focus in that teeth-gritted determination to realise an ambition kind of way, rather it's a clarity about
what's important to him and just as crucially what isn't. Much in the
same way that he dislikes food that is submerged in fripperies, he
has no time for the spun sugar webs of fussing and fighting that can
tangle up some kitchens. 'Not my cup of tea,' he says. The obvious
answer was to leave. Typically he did the straightforward thing and
said his goodbyes.

If you're getting the impression that Shaun Hill is some kind of
saint at the stove, that's probably because that's the way I tend to
think of him. A kind of guardian angel of all that's important in
good cooking, an enemy of meaningless pretension on the plate, the
reclusive, seldom-seen leader of the quiet revolution in British pro-
vincial cooking, marshalling the forces for good in our kitchens with
an unseen hand. The fact that he probably wouldn't recognise this
is part of the point; he is an accidental leader just doing what he
believes in and asking no one to follow him – except the chefs from
the Capital that is.

'I then did what I now realise was behaving badly ... I was popular
among the crew at the Capital at the time and everybody wanted to
come with me, so I took more or less a shift and this went down very
badly indeed.'

Losing a good chef is troublesome, losing an important chunk
of a good team at the same time is close to disaster. It can leave a
horrible hole that can't easily be filled, the smooth path of continuity
is fractured and the rebuilding process can be lengthy and fraught.

As a consequence, it's one of those things that's frowned upon in the trade as being just not cricket. Nevertheless, it happens all the time because it's such an easy answer. Finding good chefs whom you can work with is painfully hard so the temptation to take with you the ones you know is strong. Every time a head chef leaves rumours abound as to who's going with them, it's one of the chef's strongest bargaining cards – losing the general is one thing, losing the army quite another.

Hill led his troops to Blakes, a hotel in Fulham where he was taken on to open the new restaurant. Created out of two Victorian mansions in South Kensington by Anouska Hempel, the actress turned hotelier and designer, it was arguably the model for the fashionable small hotel in London, a discreet refuge for the rich and famous. There was no fanfare and no blaze of PR – partly because the licensing complications meant they were limited in what they were supposed to offer. But although this was a relatively low-key stop-gap for Hill, the blueprint fitted well with his style of cooking – they didn't want anything too grand but the kind of comforting regional cooking that these people would be familiar with from their travels around Europe and their villas in the South of France.

It was relaxed and fun. He had a top-class team of chefs from a Michelin-starred kitchen working with him on the kind of food that he enjoyed and he was pleased with the standard of food they were offering. There were other things to consider though, most notably that his London career wasn't doing much for his family. He still couldn't afford to buy a house and he and Anja had found themselves living in steadily crummier parts of the city. Worried about the children, he took the decision to get out of the smoke and head for the countryside.

☆ ☆ ☆

In the late seventies and early eighties the country house hotel phenomenon was spreading across the countryside like a rash. Bad attacks of chintz could soon be found throughout the land, in the company of other soon to be familiar symptoms – heavy oak panelling, stiff service, sherry in the bedrooms, most common among them. Such establishments came to occupy the space at the top end of the accommodation market in the provinces outside London and were heavily targeted at North American customers. Although mostly individually owned, they shared many characteristics and there was, and is, a sense that one is pretty much like another. Partly this was a simple response to the market, the customers they were seeking liked these kind of things. Partly, though, these shared traits reflect the straitjackets of the requirements of the tourist boards and the motoring organisations in their grading systems. They have their own view of what constitutes a top-level hotel, and if a business wants to be recognised as such then their requirements have to be met. Which means that, like it or not, they're forced into doing the same things. Some of these things are good, some of them invite ridicule.

Here's a true story. A hotel in Wales, a stylish and luxurious venue that cost several million pounds to develop, was under consideration for five-star status with the Welsh Tourist Board. In almost all aspects it had satisfied the requirements of the Welsh Tourist Board inspectors, except for two apparently crucial matters: they weren't 'presenting the napkin' at dinner and they weren't using fish cutlery. The Welsh Tourist Board refused to award five stars until these matters were addressed. The hotel didn't want to do these things, not because they didn't have the resources to do them but because they didn't like either of these practices. 'Presenting the napkin' means putting it on the lap of the customer after they sit down. Quite why this is necessary I've never worked out. I mean, it's no effort, is it? It's hardly a burden to lift your napkin from the table and place it on your own lap, and frankly, despite having experienced it many hundreds of times, I've never been comfortable with waiting staff having their hands that near to my groin – not while at the dinner table anyway. Fish cutlery is almost as pointless – those knives were designed to take fish off the bone and it's rarely served that way in restaurants today. Try to use them for anything else, like cutting, and they are worse than useless. So why bother with them? Well, if you're a potential five-star hotel in Wales you'd better get used to the idea because, however great the rest of your product is, it won't be good enough for the tourist board unless you stuff squares of white linen into people's crotches and provide customers with a redundant piece of ironware.

Notwithstanding the starchy service, the floral prints and the fish cutlery, the burgeoning of country house hotels brought plenty of positives. Home-made biscuits in the bedrooms, king-sized beds, and the opportunity to stuff the suitcase with expensive toiletries chief among them, but most of all they were, for quite a while, the home of much of the decent cooking outside London. It was quite natural then, that having decided to get out of London, Shaun Hill should find himself in one of these establishments. Ultimately, he would make his name in a country house hotel – but not this one.

The Lygon Arms is one of the grandees of country house hotels. The Savoy group bought it in 1986 for almost £5 million but prior to that it was owned by the Russell family and managed for many years by the Australian Douglas Barrington. Hill joined during the final years of the Russell ownership.

'Country house hotels were the coming thing. I'd been to Chewton Glen and Gravetye Manor and places like that to eat and I thought, that'll do me, and so I did a very dumb thing, because I do dumb things, this is not a series of smart moves. I took [a job] at what was one of the most famous country house hotels, they'd decided they wanted to join this thing [of having greater ambition for the food] and I joined as head chef at the Lygon Arms in Broadway. The chef who was there before had been there since school, thirty-nine years, and he got dumped. *Out* to make way for me. Most of the brigade had been there about fifteen years and I was about as popular as bubonic plague ... thought of as "Mr Smart-ass" coming to change every-thing, and I found myself in the odd [situation] where they wanted to change things, but they didn't want to actually do anything about it.'

The food at the Lygon took Hill back to the beginning of his career, the short-cut 'faked up haute cuisine' of margarine instead of butter, gravy browning and stock cubes. To do everything properly was inevitably going to cost more – a complication that hadn't occurred to his managers. 'They were recycling bits of old roasts and things, and all that had to go. To replace it without changing the prices or the amount that's offered means that things get difficult. You start to make things properly and initially it costs more. The brigade did their very best for me and the food moved from being quite dire to being acceptable. But it was the only time I found myself to be almost alone, the brigade did their best [and] I really liked Douglas Barrington [the general manager] but I don't think he had any palate at all. I served up some kidneys once and his had a piece of string on it which he ate rather than show other people it was there. All that amazed me at the time was that he could tell the difference.'

It was a mistake, but he was no longer in London. Changing jobs didn't just mean getting off at a different tube station, the kids had been put into new schools and he'd bought a house. He looked around the other hotels in the area but they held no hope, they even fell short of the point at which he had started his career in North London. As a distant daydream, he had thought of one day owning his own restaurant. In coming to the Lygon Arms, he'd dug himself a deep hole with few routes out – in the absence of anyone decent to work for, the only option was to work for himself.

'I decided I'd buy a restaurant ... I know that you can make things happen, if you're determined. This was an uphill struggle because I had no money, nothing in the bank. No assets except a cheap house and a car that wasn't fully paid for yet. So I looked around to find a place that was within driving distance and eventually there was a French restaurant, the health people had closed it, on the outskirts of Stratford-upon-Avon. They wanted £30,000 for it and the kitchen needed putting right. It needed £62,000 in total, and I then set about trying to borrow that.'

Given his lack of capital, this was going to require some imagination. First of all he put the best possible spin on the prospects for the new business with ridiculously optimistic cash flow forecasts 'showing that we were going to let every table three times a night and everybody was going to pay up lots and lots of money and our biggest problem would be finding enough cupboards to stash the notes in ... They all saw through that really quick.' He was turned down by all the banks, including the local Barclays, but the manager of a bigger branch of Barclays was something of a fan of his food. He came to see the premises, decided it might work and offered the loan on the condition that Hill found £7,000 of his own money to put in. Shaun Hill didn't have the £7,000 but he knew a man who did. It represented a week's takings of a sandwich bar in Leadenhall Street. Hill borrowed the money from the owner, put up his £7,000 and received the loan. 'I then wrote two cheques. One for the lease and the other for his £7,000 back ... I had to tell them [the bank] what I'd done because otherwise, evidently, it's not legal. They were really bad-tempered about it and it really soured the relationship thereafter.'

The restaurant did 'nicely', but he reckons that he didn't manage it too well. As always, he was driven by the quality of the food and this meant that he was spending rather more on the ingredients than could be justified by the prices he was able to charge. 'I'd always much rather buy a truffle or something that I'd seen in really good condition and grate it on food that's not priced up to cover it, instead of trying to get rid of three pieces of old chicken that were hanging about … and that's a fault in a lot of respects.'

When he's saying this, it's pretty clear that deep down he doesn't consider it to be a fault at all. He had no choice but to do it that way because that is the way that he's built and it's the foundation on which his cooking is constructed. It might not have been economic at the time, and the market may not have been there to support it, but taking any other approach was not an option. He might as well have given up cooking and found an alternative career. The other obstacle to success was the lack of weekday trade. He could do forty or fifty covers at the weekend but a Wednesday night in the winter might deliver a solitary table of four. With the same overheads to pay, and full-time staff employed to cover the busy nights, that made the financial equation precarious. He persisted for two years but eventually took the decision to close.

'It didn't go bust but after a couple of years it was losing money and I was worried about it … It was a limited liability company but I wanted to pay people, I didn't want people to lose out, so I closed it and sold it on. I didn't sell it and then move away like some sensible people might, I closed it, moved away and then sold it … Three ladies bought it to do old English food and that lasted no time at all … It's a Balti house now.'

The truth seems to be that it was just a few years ahead of its time. Hill enjoyed it and the food was 'as good as anything that I've ever done. It amuses me now to think that we struggled to get people to pay a few quid for dishes that people now pay large sums for, cooked by the same person.' The place was well thought of, attracting actors from the Royal Shakespeare Company ('I got to know exactly how long all of Shakespeare's plays were and I came to hate *Hamlet*, because they wouldn't come in until nearly twelve o'clock.') and garnering some positive reviews, but none of this was enough to sustain the way he wanted to cook with the emphasis on top-quality fresh ingredients. If the people weren't coming in sufficient numbers then things would go to waste; his style required a busy restaurant, every night.

☆☆☆

Although the crowds hadn't come, the Stratford restaurant had a band of avid supporters. The loyalists included Paul Henderson, the owner of Gidleigh Park, an exclusive country house hotel on the northern edge of Dartmoor. Set in forty-five acres of magnificent secluded gardens and woodland on the North Teign River, within Dartmoor National Park, the hotel is in an enchanting location. The late poet laureate Ted Hughes was a regular visitor and was moved to pen a poem in Gidleigh's honour.

Henderson asked Hill to become the new head chef at Gidleigh. '… I knew Henderson as a customer anyway and he'd been lobbying me to come through the wine merchant Bill Baker who supplied us.' Hill decided to up sticks and take the job. Perhaps for the first time, he made the move with a very specific plan in mind: he'd stay long enough to get himself straight financially and then he'd look to set up on his own again. He stayed for nine years – 'It was the first time I'd had a plan. And it didn't work.'

Partly that was because it took him some time to get on his feet and really get started. Taking on Gidleigh Park was never going to be an easy task for the independently minded Hill. First of all he was walking into a restaurant that served quite different food to his. The man he replaced, John Webber, had been a sous chef with the Swiss chef and restaurateur Anton Mosimann and naturally Webber cooked very much in the Mosimann style. This was not something Hill could or would have wanted to reproduce, and when the many returning customers came expecting the studied exactness of John Webber they were disappointed to find their favourite dishes no longer on the menu.

There was a second problem. Kay Henderson, Paul's wife, had always effectively been joint head chef, and Hill, with his experiences at the Capital still fresh in his mind, could not see how the kitchen could be run with two people in charge. 'I'm not bossy but I don't do food by committee and I had my own views on how I wanted the food to look and taste so that was a difficult one ... There was a story which Kay now backs away from of [her] departure from the kitchen. She said I was the rudest man she'd ever met and I said, "That can't be true because you're married to him."'

Paul Henderson is indeed a forceful character, but it was this single-mindedness that got Hill the appointment in the first place. 'All credit to Henderson, it was his choice. A lot of people in the trade had told him not to take me, that I was a bad idea ... because I was troublesome – which just goes to show that you can never believe [what you hear] because I've never been troublesome.'

In fact, besides his obvious talent at the stove, Hill had established a reputation for hard work and commitment. His relationship with previous bosses had rarely been explosive but it's not difficult to see that those without a real understanding of what makes good food might interpret his reluctance to compromise as an awkward streak. 'I'm not particularly rude ... but what you see [with me] is what you're going to get. Because I'd not always got on with the management at the Lygon, all the Relais and Chateau [a marketing group for exclusive hotels including Gidleigh Park] style places had listened to the management saying what a difficult ass I was and what a terrible time they were having ... and they did have a terrible time because the place was a cynical rip-off for Americans and an unpleasant travesty of what a coaching inn ought to be ... it could have been a million times better ... and I mentioned that a few times.'

Just to be helpful.

Paul Henderson seemed to appreciate that Hill was by then very sure of his own style and wasn't about to be pushed into cooking any other way. 'I knew exactly what I wanted to cook and Henderson was easy with that. And we did it, and it did very well.'

Eventually. Gidleigh Park already held a Michelin star at this point, but in contrast to his experience at the Capital, his employers weren't chained by the worry that if they changed things they might lose it. Hill had his idea of where the cooking should go and he had the support of Henderson – the retention of a Michelin star wasn't going to be a driving force. 'I've never worked either for guides or for journalists. That's not because of any disdain – I'd much prefer to have a good rating than a mediocre one – but it's a question of what you're pitching for and that has to be personal, you have to be working towards what you think is a good product for the money, the best you can do within the circumstances. When you've arrived at it then you stop. If you think that by doing it differently you'll appeal to any guide then you're moving on to territory where you're not sure what the goal is. You're second-guessing what somebody else is thinking ... you mustn't have your success or failure in life dictated by somebody else, especially a guidebook.'

Sure enough, Michelin removed the star. It's a testimony to the strength of Shaun Hill's belief in what he was doing that he could be relatively sanguine about the loss. Although Hill's detached attitude is the wisest and ultimately the most fruitful approach to the pronouncement of the critics, it's easier said than done. Michelin's awards are high-profile blessings within the industry, and to win a star can bring great acclaim, while to lose one, justified or not, is just as notable a rebuff. Hill admits that "It gave a wonderful opportunity for schadenfreude among those who think you're a loudmouth asshole.' It's easy to see how the hopes and fears stirred by the annual publication might drive a chef to try to anticipate the whims of the inspectors, but it can be little more than conjecture. As we've seen, the reasoning behind the decisions is known only to Michelin themselves and that vacuum is filled with mythmaking of the industry's own devising.

Hill did take one particular Michelin fable and turn it around for his own ends, though. 'Part of the folklore about Michelin is that once they dump you, there's no way back, and that's the end of it. You can forget about them, so,' he says cheerily, 'I did.'

In fact, Hill himself says he would have removed all of the 'gongs' that first year if he'd been in the shoes of the various guides. It was 'a shaky start' with both Gidleigh Park and Hill having to do some adjusting before things began to move forward. Oddly, the Michelin star was removed after a couple of years, just when he felt things were beginning to go well (there is sometimes a long delay between an inspection and the publishing of a change to the rating). As it turned out, this was the turning point. The decision provoked some reaction from other chefs and critics who strongly supported Hill's efforts at Gidleigh. In addition he started to receive some really good reviews, not least from Jonathan Meades in *The Times*, and he was considered part of a new wave of chefs emerging at the time, such as Rowley Leigh and Alistair Little, who had a similarly earthy and honest approach to their cooking. Whatever the pronouncements of Michelin, Hill's star was rising.

In the mid to late eighties there were the stirrings of things to come as far as television cookery was concerned. Hill was asked to do *Hot Chefs*, a morning programme for BBC1 that gave a start to the likes of Gary Rhodes, the River Café's Rose Gray and Ruth Rogers and Antony Worral Thompson among others. He also did a regular weekly spot for local television which tested his patience by requiring virtually a day's shooting for a four-minute slot.

'I didn't enjoy it. So I knocked it on the head. I've done little bits of telly but very few and it always astounds them that you're not interested, always knocks them out, they can't take it! They think it's a negotiating position. I mean, I will do things, I can be a real tart, say one thing and do another, but I don't seek them out ... because it's a different skill and I don't wish to be told when I'm supposed to be enthusiastic ... I don't want to do game shows; it's not snobbery it's just not what I want to do, I couldn't care less if people enjoy it or people want to do it. Good luck to them.'

Once again he had chanced upon an opportunity, been curious enough to take a bite and then decided firmly that he didn't much like it. Nevertheless his screen appearances were part of a general upward curve that saw his status rise among his peers, critics and ultimately guidebooks – the Michelin star was regained. Most importantly, he did well with the customers too. His food was accessible and not overwrought; often it involved doing quite familiar dishes extraordinarily well and that is *always* a good way to please people. This was the kind of cooking that pleases a broad audience, and with Hill in the kitchen Gidleigh Park went from strength to strength.

In 1993 the *Caterer and Hotelkeeper* awarded Shaun Hill its Chef Award, an accolade that is deliberated upon by a panel of industry worthies and previous winners. Whatever your view of the worth of this kind of award there's little doubt that within the catering industry it's the accolade given the highest regard by chefs. It reflected the success of Hill's years at Gidleigh Park, where he had finally found the right canvas and made his distinctive mark on British cooking. But the relationship was about to end. The stay at Gidleigh had been conceived as a temporary arrangement, a stop-gap between restaurant ventures. As it turned out, it was less of a stop-gap and more of a nine-year sabbatical, but it would, as intended, be sandwiched between adventures in the restaurant trade.

'I'd done as much as I could inside the set-up. I don't have any problem with redoing dishes, I tend to hone them and work on them … but I sort of found I'd done all I was going to do at Gidleigh, I no longer had the buzz and it was time to go.'

☆☆☆

But Hill had no idea where. He did know that he wanted to make the exit as clean and as free of controversy as possible. The world of catering, like much else, is awash with gossip and rumour. When straightforward things happen there are plenty of people around with nothing better to do than twist the tale into a more interesting shape. Chefs are constantly rumoured to be leaving one place and heading for another and an amicable exit, as Shaun Hill's was, is rarely going to be accepted on face value. So he went to Paul Henderson and they agreed to plan his departure together by announcing his leaving and then going about the business of finding a replacement. It was a neat way to move on, except in one crucial aspect – he wasn't sure what his next move would be.

He entertained the idea of a brasserie operation, toyed with converting a derelict pub, but eventually settled on Ludlow in Shropshire and the Merchant House. On the surface a far from obvious choice and besides overcoming planning difficulties and the inevitable financial hurdles he also had to hold firm against a barrage of helpful advice – most of it negative.

'The Earl of Bradford [a London restaurateur] said, 'Shropshire people won't spend that kind of money,' and it's true that chefs that have done well on the fancy-grub circuit don't cut a lot of ice out here … or didn't. But on the other hand, the whole thing was to keep it small. I mean to fill six tables, that's not asking a lot.'

Size is the key to much of the success of the Merchant House. The guiding principle is that Hill cooks food that pleases him, with the hope that it will please other people enough so that they fill his restaurant. Predictably, it does, and there is rarely an empty table to be seen on any of the five evenings and two lunchtimes each week that the Merchant House is open. The twenty-four seats, and the limited four choices for each course on the menu, are one half of the equation. The other side of the calculation is that there are only four members of staff – Hill, his wife, Anja, a single waiter and a pot-washer. The secret of their success is the way that they make the most of these limited resources. 'I try and set the menu just the right side of what is possible,' says Hill. 'The aim is to get the most that is realistic from our particular set-up. Inevitably, if that's your objective, it makes for a tense business and, for me, that's where the showmanship comes in. That's the challenge.'

There is another enormous upside to this self-reliance. It means that he has complete control over the quality of the cooking, and a degree of independence rarely found in a Michelin-starred kitchen. 'It means I have only myself to blame, which is a bit frustrating,' he lies. 'I don't have the option of being stern with a commis or bawling at the kitchen porter.' It means no recruitment problems, either, which is another potential headache eliminated. 'Getting crew can be desperately difficult, but fortunately I'm sheltered from all that,' he says. 'The problem is that there is a tendency to think the job is just about arranging things on a plate, and there is much less enthusiasm for doing the washing-up. That is perceived as something students do for a bit of extra cash.'

Until recently, when he indulged in an extra pair of hands, washer-up was another of his guises. He may be celebrated by the guides, acclaimed by the critics and revered by other chefs, but he sees nothing odd about donning the Marigolds at the end of service. 'I'm still here and there's little else to do at that point, so I might as well do it,' he says. 'It's as simple as that.'

Hill as he is fond of saying, has never have had any grand plan and yet by luck, judgement or instinct he has made a pretty good job of leaving his own, very individual mark on the map of culinary Britain. Has any restaurant had as perfect a biography as The Merchant House? A modest house becomes a diminutive restaurant and then for almost a decade, is celebrated and loved to the point where it is near impossible to secure a table. And then, in early 2005 Shaun Hill brings it all to a swift and neat end. He simply closes it – the restaurant is gone and the Jacobean building becomes a home once again. A stranger to the place might take some convincing that it was ever there – 'see that little house? It was once home to the fourteenth best restaurant in the world ...'

Happily, this is not to be the end of Shaun Hill's winding road through the restaurant trade. Even whilst planning the demise of The Merchant House he was entertaining the idea that he might 'start another catastrophe somewhere nearer population' and that has now come to fruition in a move to Worcester and a significantly larger (100-cover) restaurant. I have a feeling it's the kind of disaster the people of that cathedral city will be happy to endure.

MARCUS WAREING

Fear is a Man's Best Friend

In the entire room, only one male guest had defied the black tie dress code. At the time I assumed it was unintentional, that he hadn't read the invitation properly or had simply left it too late to order a dress suit. Whatever the reason he seemed relaxed about it and I was left envying him his ungiftwrapped state. If it had been me I wouldn't have had the courage to stay and, anyway, I was nervous enough as it was.

Marcus Wareing was sitting one seat away from me, his wife, Jane, sandwiched between us. He was wearing a light grey suit and pale blue tie, and even if the rest of the men hadn't been uniformly draped in black and white, it would still have been noticeable attire. It looked as if he'd been forced to wear it – like a gawky teenager in his dad's second suit at a family celebration. I had met him before but only once, a few weeks earlier, when I felt it necessary to approach him at a conference and express my embarrassment at the incident that had occurred at his Petrus restaurant (you'll need to have read the Preface). One of those remote apologies, where you neither did the guilty deed nor had any influence over its occurrence, but it made you squirm anyway. It was like saying sorry for the behaviour of a drunk uncle at a wedding.

I had thought that episode would have been forgotten by then, the drunk uncle would have woken sore-headed, remorseful, probably embarrassed, mumbled his apologies and let the incident disappear into history. Indeed, as far as Marcus Wareing was concerned, it was over and he never mentioned it that night. I knew differently but didn't refer to it either.

These were the 2002 Cateys, the catering industry's mock-Oscar night held by *Caterer and Hotelkeeper* magazine. Not quite Hollywood, but pitched somewhere between the Academy Awards and the British Gravel and Aggregates Producers' Annual Awards Dinner. Mary Nightingale was presenting. I was invited as editor of the *AA Restaurant Guide*, Marcus as head chef at one of London's top restaurants. I was edgy – the arguments were still going on back in Basingstoke, but I clung to a fragile thread of hope that it would all turn out okay in the end.

It was no coincidence that I was seated with Marcus Wareing; there were about a thousand people there, the odds were against it. A couple of people at the *Caterer* knew exactly what was happening and they were sitting on the story, awaiting the final outcome. I had gone to Amanda Afiya, the editor of the 'Chef' section, a couple of weeks before and in confidence, told her what was happening. I was scared that if the matter reached the conclusion I feared, I would have to give up my job. I wanted to know that it would be reported accurately, that those responsible would at least have to account for their decision. I also wanted to pitch for some writing work because in a few weeks' time there was the troubling prospect of unemployment.

Never trust a journalist, I've often been told. Well, I trusted her and I wasn't let down. Besides confiding in her nearest colleague, Joanna Wood, she kept it to herself with the promise that should the whole thing be resolved then nothing would ever be published. She sat on the story for about three months with admirable restraint but the mischievous temptation to arrange for me to sit with Marcus Wareing at the Cateys was too much for her. Although it was an uneasy geography, after a few drinks I relaxed and started to enjoy it. Marcus and Jane were good company, my wife was with me, the booze was free and at least the drunk uncle wasn't on the guest list.

☆☆☆

That night cemented my decision. Amanda Afiya had been more supportive than I could have possibly hoped when I took my account to her. She seemed to care more about my welfare than about the story, which by *Caterer* standards would be a big scoop. She emphasised that even if I lost the internal battle at the AA over the rating of Petrus, I could still choose to stay on – it would be understandable given that I had a family to think about. If I chose to do so, she wouldn't print a thing, I hadn't burned my bridges, I could stay on as editor and swallow my pride. But it wasn't about pride. I couldn't have given a toss whether someone thinks they know more about good food than me or the team of inspectors trained to assess it, be they a corpulent bureaucrat, a self-satisfied top executive or a drunk uncle at a wedding. Like I said, it's not an exact science, everyone has their opinion. The problem was that this wasn't the way we professed to go about things. We told people that we made decisions based on anonymous visits by professional inspectors. That's what the chefs were told, and it had been true, up until that point.

If I had had any thought of changing my mind, of accepting the decision from above, it left me that evening as Jane Wareing talked patiently of the sacrifices they made as a family so that Marcus could achieve his goals in the kitchen. Of his starting work at 7 a.m. and finishing at 2 a.m., of seeing his ten-month-old baby on Sundays alone. True, all this was his choice, nobody was forcing him to do it, but it was done because he was serious about what he wanted to achieve. Among those objectives were five AA Rosettes, something I knew he was entitled to but that others wanted to deny him. The difference between right and wrong is sometimes blurred, but even I didn't need a Bible to spot this one. It was plain wrong.

Marcus Wareing might have made the cover of a Smiths album. He is dark haired, thin faced and wiry, and with his north-west accent mostly intact he takes you back to another era, as though he could have been plucked from one of those gritty sixties films like *Saturday Night Sunday Morning*, *This Sporting Life* or *The Loneliness of the Long Distance Runner*. A young lad emerging from a grey landscape of boys' clubs, boxing halls and early-morning jobs stacking fruit in the market. Clichéd it may be, but it's not an illusion, all of these things have featured in his past. To go with the appearance there's an uncompromising Northern rectitude – a strong sense of honour, justice and retribution, of the meaning of loyalty and courage, of the dignity of hard work and the reward that it can later bring. In short, he's tough and self-reliant and he used to be a boxer – he may look slight, but you wouldn't want to mess with him. (I was only kidding about the suit.)

He says his father was 'a workaholic', a fruit and potato merchant who spent much of his time in the warehouse where his business was based. As a schoolboy Wareing would work there, sorting the fruit and vegetables, partly for a little pocket money but mainly because it gave him the opportunity to be with his father. He describes it as the beginning of his working relationship with food, but the lessons he drew from it are more about thrift and the value of hard work. (I was tempted to write the *meaning* of hard work, but that put me in mind of something my mother used to say almost daily to me as a teenager, 'You don't know the *meaning* of hard work.' Actually, she was wrong. I did know exactly what it

151

meant, and that was why I was so keen to avoid it; what I didn't know was the *value* of hard work.)

'My main job was packing potatoes and I got paid so much for that, but most of all it kept me close to Dad and that's where I got the understanding ... that if you've got a box of apples and twelve of them are rotten you cut the rotten off, throw that away and take the rest home in a bag and give it to your mother to do something with ... but also it taught me how to work hard and that has stayed with me, stood me in good stead.'

The first brush with the food industry may have come via his father but the inclination to be a chef originated with his brother Brian, the older sibling by seven years, who had already qualified and was cooking for a living by the time Marcus entered catering college in Southport. He took a full-time course straight from school at the age of sixteen. 'It was the old City and Guilds ... which was great because it was very much like a classical apprenticeship.' He did well and stood out enough to get noticed; at a competition one of the judges pointed him in the direction of Anton Edelmann (maître chef de cuisine at the Savoy). He had an interview, got the job and started at the Savoy just a few days after his eighteenth birthday.

'The move to London was massive for me. I was from a small seaside Northern town, I didn't know where this road was leading. It was tough and there was many a time I wished I hadn't made that move, not because of the job or the hard work, it was more the fact that I was purely homesick and missed the family and because I was so close to everyone around me. You'd pick up the telephone and you'd call the family and you'd hear them all doing great and everyone's sat in the garden or whatever at the weekend and I'm sat in the middle of this f***ing city in a boys' club in Earl's Court doing my washing and ironing and sleeping, no friends, nowhere to go, didn't know anyone ... quite shit really. There was only one thing that kept me going, that was my dad who was always at the end of a telephone.'

No Sunday went by without a call home and a long conversation with his father. The work at the Savoy was long and hard and the environment could be harsh. His father took on the role of long-distance counsellor, encouraging him to stick with it, giving advice on how to deal with problems at work and listening for literally hours on end as his isolated son poured out a week's worth of worries and frustrations. For the ex-boxer, every seven days was like a magnified three-minute round, and on Sundays he'd slump into the corner where his father would play the role of trainer, talking his spirits up, giving him some instructions for the round ahead and sending him back into the fray rejuvenated.

He threw himself into the fight, compensating for his limited skills with a singular ability to endure. He marked himself out through sheer hard work and the absence of any real social life outside work meant that there was little to interfere with his dedication to the job.

'I saw myself climbing up the ladder, chef de partie came very quickly and I started taking on huge amounts of responsibility very early ... maybe too early, that was just because I was a guy that got stuck into it and I did, very much, work with my back and not with my head ... because I didn't have an understanding of food at that age, hadn't a f***ing clue but the one thing I was, was a hard worker. If I had to be in at six o'clock to get my work done, then that's when I'd be in. That's the only way I could keep up with the older chefs because they were so much more experienced than me. That's how I battled through.'

The Savoy is an enormous operation with an unequalled history in hotel dining. When the hotel opened in 1890 a 44-year-old French chef named Auguste Escoffier was taken on. Escoffier, with his flair and imagination, became a sensation, assembling a repertoire of dishes that have maintained their popularity for well over a century with little sign of waning. True, he may not have recognised or approved of every subsequent attempt at reproducing his original versions of prawns Marie Rose, crêpes Suzette, Melba toast or peach Melba (he clearly had a thing about Dame Nellie Melba), but as we know by now, if I've been doing my job, all these things can be quite brilliant if they're made with the proper care and decent ingredients (with the exception of Melba toast which is never better than eating crisp cardboard). Of course, they rarely are.

Escoffier stayed until 1898 but his legacy endured, and having charge of the kitchens at the Savoy remained among the most prestigious jobs in catering. It was only in 2003 that the job lost some of its lustre when the empire was fractured by the granting of independence to the Savoy Grill restaurant – but more of that later.

When Marcus Wareing arrived in the late eighties, the German chef Anton Edelmann was at the helm. He had been there since

1982, when he oversaw a complete redesign of the kitchen, and had established himself as the great reviver of the Savoy's food. He was a natural leader and a marvellous organiser, the key attributes in a kitchen operation of this size, and his status inspired a wide-eyed loyalty, especially in the younger staff. 'I was just besotted by what I saw. Anton Edelmann's a fantastic chef and from an organisational point of view brilliant ... From an eighteen-year-old's point of view, everything that guy touched turned to gold ... he was the leader and we followed him.'

But he was forced to follow blindly. While Edelmann had his admiration and loyalty, Wareing was less impressed with the conduct and abilities of most of the senior chefs, who showed little interest in imparting any deeper understanding to the younger man. He felt naked in the kitchen, given big responsibilities, but unsure that he had the resources to discharge them. His lack of knowledge instilled a fear in him that he was always on the edge of committing some terrible error, that he would be found out, and he had little faith that those immediately above him would be there to come to his aid.

'The thing that was really hard was the banqueting. You had your à la carte restaurant, your room service, your ten private dining rooms and you had this banqueting facility that was seven, eight, nine hundred covers, lunch *and* dinner ... so you could have to do that twice. That was pretty tough, especially when you're short-staffed. Even more so when you're not one hundred per cent sure how things work – you don't know what chervil is, you don't know what chives are or basil, believe it or not. You come from colleges where you're taught the bare minimum. You come across coriander, you come across dried herbs ... all sorts of things [you've never heard of] and you can't get your head around it ... you hit these brick walls every day and nobody's teaching you anything. I resented some of the senior chefs because they had no understanding [of food] either, they were more interested in just blasting me with hot air, that was all they could offer.'

Despite his lack of confidence in his own capabilities he could be relied upon to get things done and to not let anyone down – this seemed to matter more than his limited knowledge of what was going on. As we've seen elsewhere, the bigger the kitchen the more demarcated the job gets and it's less a case of understanding what you're doing than understanding the instructions for how to do it. Nevertheless, Wareing remains bewildered at his early progress. '... doing those twelve or thirteen hours a day was hard enough but I had this added pressure because I worked in the cold fish section. I ordered all the fish, I did all the basic fish preparation, the mousses, and having been there four, five maybe six months, I was in charge of it ... taking that responsibility. Why I have no f***ing idea, it seemed to me that I fell into that position ... I was purchasing more food than the butchery. It was a huge amount of responsibility and it took its toll on me. My hands were all swollen and cut, you'd be cracking crabs, cracking langoustines, opening oysters, you were filleting maybe eighty or ninety salmon for a banquet, turbot, maybe fifty Dover sole for the grill. Box after box after box of fish and you'd just look at the door when they were delivering them and think *when* is this going to end.'

Lonely, exhausted, sore to his bones, living in fear of impending disaster in the kitchen and not yet twenty years old, the temptation to pack it all in and return north was enormous. But the prospect of throwing in the towel was scarier still. He'd been in the ring, as isolated a place as any you'll find, and he'd been battered before, had learned how to take the hurt and yet still stay on his feet. He wasn't about to quit. 'There was no way I ever wanted to be beaten by any other chef, there was no way I was going to ever walk out on a job. It's not me, it's not what my father taught me and it wasn't what I learned in the boxing ring, I wouldn't walk away from what I had to do in there and I never turned my back on it, I hit it face on and challenged it and I learned from it. It was my family, my father and brother who kept me there, through their support.'

Discipline is a word that has always threatened me. Not just because of the now disappeared classroom connotations of canes, slippers and belts, but because it brings to mind the prospect of doing things that I'd rather avoid. I fully understand the principle of disciplining oneself to do something either for some future reward or just because it's good for the soul, but the prospect of actually forcing myself to do it just depresses me. I have dabbled with it, a bit, when I trained for months before taking an organised cycle trip across Cuba, for instance – and there, I was driven by fear, the fear that if I didn't improve my fitness, I'd get left behind and abandoned in the Sierra Maestra. (If I'd known in advance that most of the other participants were going to be there more for the rum than the ride, I probably wouldn't have bothered.) Discipline seems to come much easier to some people, they run marathons, get up at six in the morning to work out, moderate their eating and drinking habits. I'd like to mock them in that 'why don't they get a life' kind of way, but I'd be lying, I'm actually rather envious.

In the discipline stakes, Marcus Wareing at eighteen was right up at the front with the monks – and I mean the hardline ones, not the fat and rosy-cheeked gardening and real ale types. Being paid a hundred pounds per week and living in cheap accommodation meant he wasn't short of money, but he saved it. 'I'd allocate myself a little bit of spending money on my day off … it was like being in my own little military world in a way. I did my washing and my ironing on a certain day at a certain time, I went on my run at a certain time, I went to the gym at a certain time, I slept at a certain time and I ran my life like that … never went out, never had any mates, never got involved with any of the chefs in the kitchen, I wasn't interested.'

It's the kind of routine that does indeed remind you of the military or perhaps a boxer preparing for a big fight, but there's an added element, the isolation. It may have been self-imposed – he admits to being a painfully shy young man – but it was no less real, and the strict programme seems to have been designed to keep his focus away from the pain of such a solitary existence. Much like a prisoner in confinement struggling not to break.

Although he was naturally reserved, that only partly accounts for his lack of social contact. Partly it was because he preferred to devote his energies to the job, ensuring he could cope and partly it was because he didn't much care for many of his work colleagues. "[There were] a lot of hard cases, a lot of bullies and a shitload of egos or what seemed like egos to an eighteen-year-old. I look back and I just see them as an utter load of assholes … Some of them [at the Savoy] were good guys, others were backstabbers, others were just animals, and I judge them by where they are today and have I read about them? Are they one star, two star, three star? Are they cutting the mustard? Probably one and that's Giorgio [Locatelli, who was a sous chef at the time].'

He felt no need to ingratiate himself with anyone, didn't get involved in the politics of the kitchen and absorbed the blows that came his way. While he had no grand ambitions at that stage, he wanted to get on and while he was naturally reticent by temperament, when it came to furthering his career he could be as bold as brass. If he felt he was taking on more responsibility then he'd ask Edelmann for a pay rise and he wasn't prepared to miss out on other opportunities by being coy either. 'I always noticed people doing competitions there and one day I asked Anton, "If you ever think there's something you think I'm capable of doing would you consider me for it?" and within a month I was asked to be part of the Great

Britain Culinary Olympics team … Two weeks in Toronto, Canada, which at that time was fantastic. I wouldn't dream of doing it today because it was all food on silver trays, covered in aspic, it was inedible, but to an eighteen-year-old it amazed me and I was part of a British team. I brought two silver medals home – what joy that brought to my family, it was unbelievable. You'd think I'd been away and won the [real] Olympics, I swear to God it meant that much to them and to me.'

The 'if you don't ask, you don't get' approach was encouraged by his father and it would lead to a career-defining opportunity. Egon Ronay was running some kind of competition at the Savoy with teams from various other UK restaurants. One member of staff from the Savoy was asked to join each of the competing line-ups to act as a helper, running around fetching pots and pans. Wareing himself wasn't involved, but one of his French colleagues found himself assisting Michel Roux Snr of the Waterside Inn. The Waterside team duly won and a delighted Michel Roux told the French assistant that there was a job for him at his legendary restaurant if he wanted it – he didn't.

'I was absolutely gobsmacked. I was amazed that this guy could turn a Roux brother down … I went home that evening and I called Dad and I said, "You'll never believe it, this guy got the opportunity to work at the Waterside Inn, three-star Michelin and he turned it down." I was gutted because that could have been me and his words were, "What are you doing tomorrow?" I said, "I'm off tomorrow." He said, "Right, I want you to do one thing and I want you to do this for me. I want you to get up in the morning, I want you to get your best suit on, shave and make yourself look smart. If you really want something in life you go out and get it. You go and knock on the door of Le Gavroche and ask them for a job." And I did just that.'

That spark of indignation that he'd felt when his colleague had turned down the opportunity at the Waterside Inn had lit a fire that was further fuelled by his father's bold call to action. Much like Gordon Ramsay's telephone call to Harvey's, this was on the surface an almost impudent act and one that most people would have dismissed as being hopelessly optimistic – a wild punch thrown in hope and anger. Le Gavroche, with its own three stars and Michel Roux Jr (son of Albert and nephew of Michel Snr) at the helm, was firmly at the top of the culinary tree, getting in was the dream of many chefs. Wareing managed to talk to Mark Prescott, Michel Roux Jr's right-hand man, and two weeks later he received a letter offering him a job. The speculative blow had connected with great effect and it was now time to move up a weight.

☆☆☆

Edelmann greeted the news of the impending departure with animated annoyance, telling Wareing – who'd been there twenty months – that his training at the Savoy was unfinished and he should stay. It wasn't until the end of their exchange that he enquired where the young chef was going and when he heard that it was Le Gavroche his demeanour changed. 'He got up out of his chair and he shook my hand and said, "Congratulations, well done" and I thought, what a gent, what a true professional, because he admired me for going somewhere better than his own kitchen.'

Better? Well, yes. It would be a strange judgement that put the food delivered at the Savoy in the same league as the offerings from Le Gavroche. The caveat, of course, is that we're not comparing like with like. Anton Edelmann's challenge at the Savoy was to cater for enormous numbers and still maintain a high standard; at Le Gavroche the effort is focused on a much smaller operation without the distractions of mass banqueting, multiple restaurants and extensive private dining. These things need to be borne in mind when we ponder the quality of some restaurants. There are restaurants with a Michelin star that serve a tiny number of customers – I can think of at least one recipient where the guests were required to sit down at the same time and the menu was without choice – less of a restaurant and more of a paying dinner party. There's nothing wrong with that of course, and it's to be celebrated if it means that the food on the plate is of a consequently high standard. It's just a recognition that the operational imperatives of some eating places dictate what they can offer and the intelligent restaurateurs and chefs cut their cloth accordingly with the most important dictum being the larger the operation, the simpler the food should be.

At that time the Savoy kitchens were operating on an industrial scale with well over a hundred chefs employed. The atmosphere was that of a manufacturing shop floor, noisy, boisterous and with a necessary emphasis on speed of production. Entering the kitchen at Le Gavroche was like walking through a door that somehow transports you from the clatter of a city centre to a shady spot by the river. 'Calm, quiet, precision, no bedlam, no noise ... you could feel the concentration in the air. I was twenty and it was just another world in cookery, different from what I ever thought it could be.'

The introduction to the studied atmosphere of the kitchen at Le Gavroche was a defining point in itself for Wareing. That first night he rang his father elated at what he had found, at the difference in attitude of the other chefs, at the remarkable standards that ran through from the preparation of the food to the gleaming standards of hygiene. He felt instantly at ease with the levels of personal discipline demanded and the seriousness with which the chefs approached their work; instead of struggling to maintain his own focus among the chaos around him he was now part of a tight unit that shared values he could recognise. The move to Le Gavroche was a revelation and showed the direction for his future career, but it was coupled with another twist of fate that would do much to determine his path over the next decade. That same night he had something else to report to his father.

'I said, "There's twenty-two chefs in that kitchen but there is one guy in there who is so different from anyone else, he's just like obsessed. He f***s around from time to time but Dad ..." I said, "At twelve o'clock and at seven o'clock he turns into a f***ing focused cooking machine and just cleans up, just wipes the board clean."

"Listen," he said, "a guy like that, you watch him, you listen ... and more importantly you stick next to him, you might learn something." And that was him, that was Gordon, that was where we first met.'

As the sometimes dubious advice from a parent goes, it was a gem. He couldn't have known that Gordon Ramsay was on a course that would take him to the heights of his profession but some instinct told him that his son would do well to steer in his direction. The closeness to Gordon Ramsay would nourish Wareing's career in the years to come in the same way that Marco Pierre White had nurtured Ramsay's own talent. When you think about it, it's a common enough tale. Seldom does anyone achieve much without finding a mentor for at least some of the way, someone to feed off, someone to believe in, someone to journey with. Very little comes from a vacuum.

☆☆☆

If Wareing had any feeling that he was going to be eased into things at Le Gavroche, that the pressure would ease for a while, then he was in for a shock. He was put on the vegetables, taken to the cookery (rather than the preparation) part of that section and introduced to the chef running it. It would be a short acquaintance, he was leaving the following week and Wareing was told he would be replacing him. 'My ass fell out of my trousers ... there was this huge challenge right in front of me and I just had to take it on

164

board. I was just really, really nervous, the whole thing just blew me away.'

What's the fuss about? After all it was only the veg he was cooking. But this was Le Gavroche, three Michelin stars, arguably the best restaurant in the UK at the time, already a legend. It might not have been the lead role but it was crucial. To think otherwise would be like being asked to replace Charlie Watts in the Rolling Stones and greeting it with a shrug – 'No worries, it's only the drums.'

Typically, he had a ready-made solution – the trick that had got him through the early months at the Savoy. 'I worked my ass off ... Again I was in the kitchen at six o'clock and I'd be nearly en place before chef would arrive at nine. I used to get told off sometimes because all my sauces, all my fish would be organised that early. It was like military precision with me.'

Unsure of his capabilities, about how he would measure up, he took no chances. Coming in early and working the extra hours was a safety mechanism, giving him leeway should anything go wrong. He'd had less than two years in a professional kitchen and all his experience had been in the very partitioned environment of the Savoy. Unsurprisingly, he was less than confident. By contrast, Gordon Ramsay had been at Harvey's with Marco Pierre White, where he had grown used to dealing with responsibility and pressure. As a result his working style was quite different from Wareing's but from Ramsay's point of view the two approaches knitted together conveniently.

'I was so en place that even f***ing Gordon used to help himself to my section. And he did, he was a sod at times. But he did it because Gordon had worked for Marco and he could push himself and he knew his limitations [endurance wise]. I didn't know my limitations. Gordon could walk in the kitchen at eight-thirty or just before Michel came and still be en place ... Gordon was a master at letting all the people around him do his work for him. F***ing clever. I was the opposite, I wanted to do it all myself ... and he knew that, so he'd help himself and there was nothing I could do about it.' Until one day he lost patience with it and complained to Michel Roux Jr. Ramsay was duly censured but there was no long-term impact on their relationship. If anything the fact that Wareing had stood up for himself seemed to earn him greater respect.

The vegetable challenge was negotiated with relative ease and he found himself running the cooked fish section, a major step up. The rate of his progress still puzzled him, especially when his commis chef on that section was Stephen Terry, who had been a key part of the Harvey's set up for three years. It was a tense time for Le Gavroche. Michel Roux Jr had not long taken over and he was determined that standards wouldn't slip. It made him a tough taskmaster and he would countenance nothing in the way of short-cuts. 'He was very strict but, God, did he know how to cook.' Attention to detail was the key to the restaurant's success; it required exactness and it required attentiveness. There was little levity about – except from one direction. 'The only joy in that kitchen was having Gordon there. He was just a comedian, he was a guy that would do anything to distract someone ... do anything to take people's eye off the ball but yet always keeping *his* work right on line.'

There may not have been much in the way of light relief but Wareing wasn't there for the laughs. Michel Roux Jr and Mark Prescott were both accomplished chefs and great teachers. 'You started to understand a little bit more because you were being taught more ... I went on to the veg and learned how to cook that really well, then Michel put me into the bakery. I did pastry, bread and learned how to make great bread and I spent the last seven months on the hot fish and that's really where I came into the light, because I was the youngest chef de partie and the youngest there had been for a long time [at Le Gavroche]. So I was quite proud of that.'

The principle that was guiding him at that time was a simple one – if he worked hard, he'd be rewarded. There was no thought in his mind that he had some special talent, that his natural abilities would propel him forward. When he thought of the future it was in terms of the day when he wouldn't have to work this hard, when he'd have earned his passage out of the rigours of the kitchen. 'Longing for that day to get out, longing for that job that was easier, where you could work reasonable hours.' If he had developed a passion for cooking, it was still latent, it wasn't what was driving him on. Instead, his motivations were the belief that he could work his way to a better life and the fear that he might fail to face up to the challenge.

That slightly 'easier life' wasn't as far away as he might have imagined. About 3,470 miles from Le Gavroche lies the Saranac Lake in upstate New York. The Point is a luxury resort situated on the shore of the lake and comprising a series of lavish timber buildings that accommodate eleven guest rooms and a 'great hall' where guests take their meals. Albert Roux, having retired from the day-to-day running of Le Gavroche, was branching out into lucrative consultancy deals of which the Point was one and he asked Marcus Wareing to go out there.

If you were mapping out a career path for a chef who was on his way to the higher reaches of the profession, it's doubtful that you'd suggest this as a nine-month diversion. The Point was prestigious, and the reason to involve Albert Roux was to ensure that the standards were high, but it wasn't really a restaurant in the conventional sense. The resort was self-contained and, with just the eleven rooms, there was a maximum of twenty-two covers to deal with. In addition, the menu was fixed, different each night, but without choice. As anyone who has been involved in the running of a restaurant will tell you, this removes most of the biggest headaches from the operation. As a learning experience it had little merit, but that was hardly going to be at the forefront of Marcus Wareing's mind.

'At twenty, if someone puts the opportunity to go to New York in your lap, or do you want to go to France where you can't speak a word of the language, you take New York. I think back and I think what a good time I had, but who was Albert doing it for? Was he doing it for me [in terms of furthering the chef's learning] or was he doing it for himself because he needed a chef to go out there? And I think he was doing it for himself. Which is understandable, I was no different from any other chef that worked for him.'

It was by no means a holiday. He was expected to work hard, but there was the opportunity to play hard too. It was an easing of the pressure and the opportunity to relax a little. Tellingly, Wareing says he was 'part of a family ... they took you out and you started to realise there was something going on outside of the kitchen. That was the only way to get off site [given the isolated location], being taken somewhere to see a movie or have dinner or just sit alongside the lake and have a margarita in the Mexican bar. It was a really nice part of my career.'

Despite the affection for that period, it's obvious that, looking back, Wareing feels just a tinge of annoyance that he gave himself that breathing space instead of pressing on. 'Gordon looks back on it and says it's part of your career that really was a waste of f***ing time. In his eyes he may be right, but in mine it was a little bit more than that. Pretty much like what he did on the boat ... a sabbatical rather than part of the learning curve.'

Personally, I think they were both entitled to a break.

☆☆☆

The nine months in the wilderness over, Wareing headed for yet another Albert Roux consultancy project. It had been intended that he'd go to the ski resort of Isola but as the result of crossed wires he ended up in Amsterdam where a Café Roux was opening at the Grand Amsterdam Hotel. He spent a few months there working under Stephen Doherty, a former head chef at Le Gavroche, concentrating his efforts on pastry and bakery. By then he was becoming conscious of the gaps that he needed to fill in his knowledge – the trouble was, he wasn't entirely sure of how to go about filling them. Holland didn't appeal to him and he looked to get back to Britain, but London too had temporarily lost its allure, and in the absence of any obvious options he called an old colleague from Le Gavroche, Max Gnoyke, who was working at a country house hotel in West Sussex called Gravetye Manor. By chance, Gnoyke was about to leave and encouraged Wareing to apply for his post as a chef de partie. Wareing did so and got the job.

He made an instant impression and in a matter of months was promoted to sous chef, the highest rank he had so far held. Of course, Gravetye wasn't Le Gavroche, but nevertheless the owner, Peter Herbert, was not short of ambition for the restaurant. Wareing's position meant that for the first time he had some input into the composition of the food and contributed a number of dishes to a tasting that had been called to assemble a new menu. Herbert was impressed and excited by the food that Wareing delivered.

Wareing was less energised though; he'd lost a little direction. It wasn't that he disliked Gravetye Manor, and as a country house hotel it provided a variety of accommodation for the young staff so there was consequently a lively social scene which he took full advantage of. In the kitchen, the head chef, Stephen Morey, was a capable cook and an affable personality who worked 'ridiculously hard … as hard as the rest of the brigade put together. He'd do everything if they let him and the thing was, they pretty often did.' But the ardour had dimmed. Gravetye was a comfortable place to be and compared with his earlier experiences offered little in the way of a challenge. The fear had gone and taken the fire with it.

It was the aromas of London that eventually stirred him. The team at Gravetye were joined by a chef who had just left the Canteen, Marco Pierre White's second restaurant venture, which had just picked up its first Michelin star. 'This guy started talking about the whole Marco thing and this amazing food with a real passion … and I caught it … Suddenly I could feel the buzz again and I thought, this is just too interesting to be away from. I've go to do something about it. I've got to get back to London.'

The big news from the capital was that Pierre Koffman had got three stars for his restaurant La Tante Claire. As a thank you to his team he brought all the staff to Gravetye in a clapped out old bus and treated them to a celebratory lunch of steak and kidney pudding. When service was over Wareing went for his customary five-mile run and then fell asleep, returning to the kitchen twenty minutes late. 'He'd been in the kitchen. Just won three stars, that was massive, this was a really big chef and I missed the opportunity to shake his hand … I was so pissed off.'

He had been contemplating a return to North America to take up a sous chef's post that had been offered to him in Vermont, but the visa was taking an age to come through. In the meantime, the missed opportunity to meet Koffman gnawed away at him. He was ready to leave Gravetye but the delay with the visa meant that he was marking time and London was still calling him. He asked Stephen Morey to organise a *stage* at La Tante Claire and made the short journey north back to the city.

★ ★ ☆

Fate ...

'Pierre Koffman introduced himself and took me downstairs to the changing room and I heard this almighty laugh coming from the fridge. I thought, f**k me, I recognise that laugh, then the door comes bursting open and it's him! I couldn't believe it, I hadn't seen him for three years and it's f***ing Gordon. And he's like, "What the f***ing hell are you doing here?" Koffman just stood there bewildered saying, "You know each other?"'

Koffman's three stars had brought him legendary status in the culinary world. By some omission, I never went to La Tante Claire in its Royal Hospital Road incarnation but I did twice visit the later, quite short-lived version in the Berkeley Hotel, Knightsbridge. The first time was a routine inspection for the *AA Restaurant Guide* that would contribute to assessing its rating in the next book. The second time, just a few weeks later, was to see if it really could be that bad twice. It was.

This guy had three stars. That didn't happen by accident, and I know from other people's experiences that he served some outstanding food at Royal Hospital Road. I just didn't get any at the Berkeley, that's all. Partly it's about expectation, but even if I hadn't been antici-pating something special, those would have been mediocre meals with basic flaws – tired ingredients, overcooking and clumsy seasoning. I have no idea why this should have been, but there was one other incident that occurred during the first meal that made me wonder whether the customer wasn't being treated as less than sentient. I was with a colleague and we ordered a bottle of wine, something the AA expenses allowed only at the more highly rated restaurants. It was a bottle very much from the lower priced end of the list. You get used to ordering that way as an inspector and it stands you in good stead for the rest of your life. Once you've been into a smart restaurant, contemplated the doorstop of a wine list and picked from the handful of sub-£25 bottles a few times, you get over the embarrassment of thinking the sommelier is sniggering at you.

And there are a few sniggerers about. The wine arrived and it was tainted, quite clearly, not drinkable. Politely (of course) I sent it back. The sommelier returned moments later. 'The wine isn't a hundred per cent, sir, but there's nothing actually wrong with it.'

'I don't understand?'

'It's not perfect, sir, but then ... I can find no fault with it. Never-theless, if you are not happy, I will change the bottle.'

173

The new bottle arrived. Compared to the first offering it was shinier, richer in colour and the musty aroma of the first bottle had been replaced by a lively scent of red fruit. There was absolutely no comparison between the two. The waiter poured a tiny amount and sniffed it himself. 'There is a slight difference, sir, a nuance.'

I wanted to hit him.

Ramsay's presence was the trigger for Wareing to refocus his sights. 'Pierre Koffman, three stars, Gordon Ramsay as sous chef, this is for me. F**k America, f**k Gravetye, I was out ... I said, "Chef [to Stephen Morey], what do you think?" He said, "Go for it." I left, I was down to London in a month. On the very first morning of starting the job I walked into the kitchen and I thought, Gordon, where's Gordon? Nine o'clock he arrives and I said, "Bloody hell, you're a bit late, mate. Nice to see you haven't changed your tune," and he goes outside and spends an hour with Koffman. He's only giving his f***ing notice in to Koffman! I'm thinking, you bastard. I said, "I've just f***ing come here to work under you." Because I knew what he was like, I knew how good he was going to be.'

There's nothing quite like that empty feeling of having your hopes dashed, is there? That phrase about having 'the wind taken out of your sails'. How true is that? Isn't that exactly how it feels? I once wrote an article for the *Sunday Mirror*, who had offered me £1,000 to go to McDonald's, Harry Ramsden's and the like. They even sent a photographer with me. I'll eat anywhere for £1,000, even at those places. I went, wrote about them and compared them unfavourably to local independent businesses in the same market. It wasn't a hatchet job, just honest ... honest. The people at the *Mirror* said they loved it and I couldn't wait for the Sunday papers to arrive, so I drove to a local newsagent at six in the morning. I got back into the car and rifled through the pages without finding the article. I tried again, this time including the sport section. Nothing, they didn't print it, and I never found out why. They paid me but that wasn't my real concern, I had thought I was going to be published in a national paper and suddenly I wasn't.

Ramsay left within the week, leaving Wareing behind at La Tante Claire. His departure was a horrible blow. Wareing's return to London had been inspired as much by the chance to work with Ramsay as by the opportunity to re-enter a three-star kitchen. The disappointment would have been less acute if La Tante Claire had matched his expectations, but it didn't. 'Three-star kitchen! This guy didn't tell you anything. He didn't tell you what the lunch menu was, he didn't tell you where to get anything. The lunch menu would go on the wall at ten thirty – "Make sure you're ready by twelve" ... it was just unbelievable, sixty-five dinners, forty-five lunches every day, and you didn't know if you were coming or going and you thought, this is not right. I couldn't click with the man ... he was more interested in bollocking me for the staff salad than for the [restaurant] food

... I thought, I don't want to work here, I really don't like this ... I couldn't click with Koffman, didn't like his attitude.'

Gordon Ramsay had told Wareing of his plans for Aubergine and given him the address. One night after service he made his way from La Tante Claire to 11 Park Walk, also in Chelsea. It was a grim, wet night and by then it was past one o'clock in the morning. He found a side door and a staircase leading down, slipped and stumbled clumsily through the door into the kitchen. 'In the kitchen were Gordon, Stephen Terry, Marco Pierre White and Tim Payne ... Marco with all that hair all over the place and by this time he was a legend ...'

Famous and notorious at the same time, Marco Pierre White was an intimidating figure to be unexpectedly confronted with, especially for the first time. Wareing remembers the subsequent exchange as follows.

MPW (with disdain): Gordon, who the f**k is this? (All the cold air was coming in via the door that Wareing had pretty much fallen through.) Close the f***ing door, will you?

(MW closes the door.)

MPW: Come here ... what's your f***ing name?

MW: Marcus Wareing.

MPW: Marcus is a bit of a posh f***ing name, isn't it? Where do you work?

MW: La Tante Claire.

MPW (with relish): It's *shite*, isn't it?

MW: It's all right.

MPW: Do you think you're a good chef?

MW: Well, yeah, I'm all right.

MPW: Do you work hard?

MW: Yeah.

MPW: Do you want a job?

MW: Er … yeah!

MPW: Well, be here tomorrow at eight o'clock and don't be f***ing late. F**k Koffman, don't worry about him.

As he walked back on to the rainy street in the early hours of the morning, his father's words about sticking close to Gordon Ramsay echoed in his mind. Fired up with excitement, he called him again. 'You go for it,' his father told him, 'you've got nothing to lose.'

The following day he returned to that kitchen as White had instructed, and his life changed for good. Gordon Ramsay was striking out on his own, much in the way that Marco Pierre White had done at Harvey's, and Wareing was set to play the same part that Ramsay had played for White. It would be the most demanding of roles.

☆☆☆

For the next two years Marcus Wareing gave the bulk of his life to Aubergine and more directly to Gordon Ramsay. As sous chef, second in command, he was expected to open the kitchen at 6.45

a.m. and would rarely leave before 1 a.m. the following day. A couple of months before starting at 11 Park Walk, he had embarked on a relationship with a colleague at Gravetye. Jane would later become his wife, but during the Aubergine period he would rarely see her apart from Sundays when he'd finish Saturday-night service, take an early morning train to Gatwick and get a taxi to Gravetye, usually arriving at 4 a.m.

The extraordinary intensity of the work at Aubergine was far greater than anything he'd encountered and the responsibility of being Ramsay's deputy just added to the weight on his 23-year-old shoulders, but these weren't the heaviest of the burdens he had to bear. '[It was] a mind-bending, mental part of my career and he [Ramsay] put me through that. The hardest part was working for a friend ... who treated me like everybody else and I found that very hard. That this friend of mine, this guy I'd been out on the piss with, been to his flat, had a laugh and a joke, taken the piss out of him because he would never teach me anything at Gavroche, never tell me his recipes, he'd say, "F**k off! Go away, when you get your own section I might tell you." This guy that was the big wind-up merchant, then I became one of *his* cooks and I found that very difficult to come to terms with. Many times I was crying inside because this friend of mine was f**king abusing me verbally ... He gave me the sous chef's job straight away and I was delighted, really flattered by that, but f**k me did I pay for it.'

It clearly hurt very badly, but Wareing would try to give no outward sign of his distress. He took the verbal beatings, regathered himself and thought of the long game. He could see Ramsay was special and that the cooking they were turning out had few peers in London and beyond. If the price was to endure the wounding abuse of his friend and mentor then he'd pay it. 'Pure sacrifice ... I wanted him to know that I would do it. There was never ever a day when he thought I wouldn't be there. I never wanted him to wake up in the morning and wonder whether Marcus Wareing would be coming to work today because he caned my arse the night before.'

Aubergine bore the imprint of Ramsay's time at Harvey's. Although the cooking was quite different (Ramsay was developing a lightness of touch and precision founded on his time at Le Gavroche and his French experiences) the culture of the kitchen had striking similarities. Ramsay, like White before him, was a man with a mission. This was a finite journey, a road to the stars and he could only navigate according to the landmarks that he knew. Hard work, discipline and an intolerance of anything less than 100 per cent commitment were the foundations on which he'd seen others build their success and, like White, he looked to band together a small team whose loyalty was undivided, who would struggle together and who would draw new strength from every setback, every vicious flurry of blows. 'Gordon didn't just teach you cookery, he taught you lots of things. We were very much a very close family and Gordon was in the kitchen every day at eight o'clock and left every morning at two o'clock, he worked like a trooper and we were all in the same boat which was nice ... He was at the front of the boat steering us but he was always there, he was never not there and you knew that, felt you were in safe hands and I respected that.'

Respect was the glue that held this potentially fragile venture together. It was respect for Ramsay's ability as a chef, his patent dedication and his sense of direction that kept his weary band of followers on board. In turn, Ramsay taught them to respect the food they worked with, to learn its nature and understand its potential. He also had a strong sense of the brotherhood of the profession, of the need to respect others that toiled in this grinding trade.

Ramsay sent a couple of chefs down to Richard Corrigan's restaurant in Fulham Road for dinner on a Sunday night when Aubergine was closed. On their return to Aubergine, Wareing remembers that Ramsay quizzed them on the meal, asking about the standard of cooking, the service, the price. '... and then he said to one of them, "Did you leave a tip?" and this guy said, "No" and Gordon went f***ing crazy. "How can you work in this industry where people work as hard as you and you don't leave a tip?" He was absolutely crazy. All the chefs around were listening and thinking, "hell". You were learning little things like that all the time, things that would change your view and your behaviour ... It was more than just cookery there.'

Day in, day out, Wareing stuck with it for two years, long enough to see Aubergine through to the first of the two Michelin stars it would achieve. It was a period of exponential growth in Wareing's ability and his confidence. 'The food there was something else. No disrespect to the other chefs I have worked under, but I thought I was a shit-hot cook before I went to Aubergine and that was because of the pieces of paper I had, what my CV showed. But that was where I learned to cook, at Aubergine, with Gordon.'

With his self-belief growing it was perhaps inevitable that his relationship with Ramsay would fracture at some point. Wareing left, first to do a *stage* in New York with Daniel Boulud (widely thought of as being among the top chefs in the USA) and then to work in France with Guy Savoy, as Gordon Ramsay had done.

'I never ever felt that I understood food until the day I left Aubergine ... Then at Guy Savoy I felt I could stand in that kitchen, after two years with Gordon ... the guy on my left, the guy on my right, the people in front of me – I did not fear any of them. I just focused on what I was doing and whatever it was, I felt so strong and confident in myself. I couldn't give a f**k if I couldn't speak French ... I just knew I could cook. It was only then that I felt good.'

Being distanced from Aubergine and Gordon Ramsay gave him the perspective to realise how far he had come. There was a real depth to his understanding of food and cooking techniques but he had also learned much about himself. Whereas he had once been propelled by the need to prove himself, driven on by the desire to take every possible step to stave off the frightening prospect of failure, he now felt a surge of faith in his ability. At the same time the break in his working relationship with Ramsay meant that their friendship was free from the stress caused by their relative roles in the kitchen. Although he and Ramsay had quarrelled and this had precipitated his departure, the fissure was soon healed.

'I had thought that was it when I left Aubergine. I assumed that part of my career was over … On the very first day I started [at Guy Savoy] the phone goes and Michel, the chef, says, "Marcus, telephone," and it was him just saying, "What's going on? How are you doing? What's happening there?" … When I left Aubergine I thought that was it and I [was about to] move on to the next stage of my life but no, he never left me alone … he was talking to me about his personal life, talking to me about my life. He was becoming my friend again.'

Wareing appreciated being at Guy Savoy, but his regular conversations with Ramsay meant the excitement and fury of Aubergine continued to resonate with him. He began to feel that he was losing out on being part of something special, something unique to the time. 'I missed him and I missed *it*.' It wasn't to be a lengthy estrangement.

☆☆☆

I'm not aware of too many geldings and there is a real shortage of mares, but the way that the restaurant industry procreates to ensure a constant supply of quality cooks is, nevertheless, a little like a stud farm. A chef comes from a top breeding ground (say, one of the brothers Roux), is put through his or her paces and if they look promising they're trained and nurtured until they make a name for themselves in their own right. They then have a few years at the top themselves, actually putting in performances on the course, before they start producing their own progeny. Partly this happens as a by-product of the simple fact that the great kitchens need a supply of excellent chefs and the only way to ensure that is to develop them. Another motivation, no doubt, is the satisfaction of seeing a chef leave your kitchen and go and make terrific food somewhere else. There is also a good deal of enlightened self-interest. As we've seen (yes, I know that by now you're just weeping at the plight of those poor chefs and restaurateurs), there's not much money in the restaurant game and one of the ways to exploit any success you have is to use your name to open up elsewhere. The trouble with that is that it's notoriously difficult to run restaurants when you can't be there all the time. Branching out is therefore fraught with difficulty, and there are plenty of examples of failure to prove the point. Nobody quite gives a restaurant the same love and attention as its owner and an owner can only be in one place at a time, I think. I'm not entirely sure about Marco Pierre White, who in the early days of putting together his mini-chain of London restaurants seemed to be present at several simultaneously. I can honestly only remember a handful of occasions when I inspected an MPW restaurant and he didn't at some point appear like Banquo's ghost, his presence a pointed reminder of just whose eating place you were sitting in judgement of. I was convinced that once an inspector was spotted (as I've said, it's not that difficult), he'd be contacted at once and would hotfoot it from wherever he happened to be at the time. Maybe I flatter myself, he probably couldn't have given a toss about the editor of the *AA Restaurant Guide*, but I do know that when he was cooking at the then heart of his little empire, the three-star Oak Room, he worked incredibly hard to keep his finger on the various pulses of his scattered offspring, dashing across London to make his presence felt at as many of his restaurants as he could before the evening was out.

One answer to this dilemma – how to expand the product without diluting the quality and damaging the brand – is to find other people who are almost as good at their job as you are and, crucially, giving them a stake in its success too. Ramsay and his business cohorts of the time, A to Z Restaurants, already had a high-profile success in Aubergine and were looking to capitalise on it. Marcus Wareing was the obvious choice for their next venture together.

'I got a phone call [from Ramsay], he said, "I'd like you to come over this weekend, there's something I'd like to show you. I'll pay for your ticket." So I went over and he took me to L'Oranger in St James Street. I didn't have a clue where I was, all I knew of London was the boys' club in Earl's Court, the Savoy, Aubergine and Gavroche. I knew nothing else. So we were there in the lobby of the restaurant and he just said, "If you want it, it's yours." Just like Marco had said to him at Aubergine. I was back.'

Taking charge of a kitchen for the first time sent Wareing into a spin. 'I had no understanding of how a restaurant should be run. I hadn't a clue how to run a kitchen, hadn't a clue how to talk to people ... didn't even know how to write a menu properly. My first menu tasting [a trial of dishes prior to opening] was a *disaster*, a total f***ing disaster and I really thought, this is not right. It was mistake after mistake.'

Back at Aubergine, the race was on to achieve a second star in the next edition of the Michelin guide and Ramsay was limited in the time he could spare to guide the novice at L'Oranger. Wareing was unsure of himself and the direction of his food, he had doubts as to his ability to make a success of the restaurant and he was nervous of failure. So he did the only thing he knew, dug deep into his well of resilience and kept getting up from every setback, refusing to give in. He looked at his performance and he was dissatisfied, critical. Others were clearly more impressed. After just seven months, in January 1997 he was awarded a Michelin star of his own, on the same day that Aubergine achieved its second. 'That was the best star I'll ever win because it was the most unexpected thing ever. I was twenty-five [younger even than Ramsay when he won his first star] and you could have knocked me over with a feather ... It was as if I'd won the lottery, it felt that good.'

But this was no lottery, no gift of chance. Wareing had been prepared to put himself into some uncomfortable situations, he'd earned his prize. When he was racked by doubt, questioning his own abilities, he still kept to the path, relentless and often isolated, like a lonely long-distance runner pressing on through pain, like a boxer on the ropes refusing to go down. Bathed in the glow of the newly acquired star, L'Oranger flourished and Wareing grew in confidence. For a couple of years it was a sparkling success story. 'L'Oranger was a money machine ... it was churning money out, spitting it out the door.' He could see what he was creating in terms of revenue but he was beginning to wonder where his share of the bounty was. 'I was promised all sorts of things but I got f**k all. I could turn that restaurant up ... I could make it make money ... I never lost them money, I always made them money, all I wanted was my cut; I was promised ten per cent and I got jack sh*t.'

The relationship between Wareing and A to Z began to splinter. Accusations flew from both sides, claim and counter-claim fizzed back and forth until finally Wareing was sacked, escorted from the premises by security and replaced by another chef. 'Suddenly, I was unemployed, gobsmacked. I felt like someone had just tipped me out of a boat, I was absolutely devastated.'

Ramsay's own relations with A to Z were similarly fraught. The senior management were keen to capitalise on the success of Aubergine and L'Oranger by floating on the stock market and expanding into a chain. Ramsay wasn't interested in rolling out concepts. A few days after Wareing's dismissal, Ramsay gave up his position as a director of A to Z and on the Monday he resigned his post at Aubergine. His forty-five staff did likewise, opting to follow the two-star chef to his new restaurant in Royal Hospital Road. The out-of-work Wareing went with them.

He spent six months at Restaurant Gordon Ramsay helping to set it on the path that would eventually lead to three stars, but his days of playing the supporting role were over. He entered into a business partnership with Ramsay and his father-in-law, Chris Hutcheson, and within six months launched Petrus in St James Street, a stone's throw from where he'd been cooking at L'Oranger. But it wasn't the proximity of his old restaurant that threatened to overshadow the new venture. The tussle with A to Z was far from over. Wareing and Ramsay were being sued.

'I got into bed with Chris Hutcheson and Gordon Ramsay … There's one thing that guy [Hutcheson] did for me that I'll never forget … He came up to me the night before we opened and he said, "Marcus … you're on the verge of making your name, doing your own thing. You've got a guy suing you … for over a million pounds, that's going to put a massive amount of pressure on your shoulders. I just want you to do one thing for me, I just want you to forget it. I want to deal with it, I just want you to cook … You do your job and I'll do mine." That's exactly what I did.'

It was a weight lifted. Wareing was able to focus on Petrus and his efforts quickly bore fruit. The food attracted praise from both newspaper critics and the guidebooks and it was no surprise when he garnered a Michelin star for the second time. In 2003 Wareing moved Petrus to the Berkeley Hotel, replacing the second incarnation of Pierre Koffman's La Tante Claire. In the same year he took on the Savoy Grill and at the same hotel opened Banquette, an informal restaurant styled after an American diner, while his first boss, Anton Edelmann, announced his departure from the hotel.

'You'll never do anything in the shadow of Gordon Ramsay,' a less than well-wisher once told Wareing. It was a cheap jibe; he may have been in the shadows, but he was punching his own weight, shadow boxing if you like. Punching and jabbing his way through the rounds to end up running the kitchens at some of the best regarded restaurants in the country, winning a Michelin star at two separate restaurants, hotly pursuing a second and being awarded the *Caterer and Hotelkeeper*'s Catey for Best Chef in 2003.

And in the 2003 edition of the *AA Restaurant Guide*? The highest award possible – five AA Rosettes, a significant accolade that put Petrus on a par with Gordon Ramsay's eponymous restaurant in Royal Hospital Road. Well, anything else would have been an injustice, would it not?

A COOKIE CRUMBLES

It was about 3 p.m. when I got the call.

Basingstoke to Carmarthen is a three-hour drive if the traffic's really friendly. Leaving immediately I could be back at the restaurant not long after six, the first table would be in at about 7.15. There were only twenty-six people booked, comprising eight tables, a moderate evening by any standards. I could cope with that surely. Within minutes I had left my desk on the seventh floor of the AA offices, hurried through the car park and begun the journey west. By the time I'd reached the junction with the M4 I was beginning to feel pretty confident, when I hit the Severn Bridge I was bullish, just outside Bridgend I began to take advance pleasure in the thought of saying goodnight to a band of happy customers eager to thank me for my impressive efforts. At Swansea I hit a six-mile tailback and began to sweat. It was gone seven when I turned into the drive; by then I felt sick.

It wasn't the first time that I had cooked for paying guests, but I had left the restaurant seven years before and the truth was that even then my presence in the kitchen had been a rarity, a last resort. My part in the partnership had been front of house, a role that over time I had carefully pared down to the essentials. Greet the guests, take a few orders, maybe carry a few plates and then, as the evening wears on, visit the tables of the customers that look happy just to check that they really are enjoying it, while skilfully avoiding any that look potentially awkward. These duties discharged, I would then feel able to sit down with some of the regulars and help them finish their wine. Meanwhile, the other two thirds of the partnership (my wife, Maryann, and my sister-in-law, Charlotte) would be in the kitchen knocking out up to fifty covers on an Aga and a domestic cooker with only a washer-up for assistance. If this seems unfair, I'd rather you kept it to yourself; there may well be a reservoir of resentment there just waiting to be tapped. And anyway it was just a fact of life that I happened to be good at dispensing good cheer and liberal measures, while they happened to excel at cooking, organisation and hard work. I can't help it if I'm lucky.

Despite the meagre staffing levels, the occasions when I was called into the kitchen were few and far between. By necessity, illness was a stranger to either of the girls, and even when it did visit, they'd struggle through almost any complaint. In fact, in the seven years since I'd given up taking an active role in the restaurant it had never really occurred to me to consider what they would do if one of them was taken sick. Now I knew. Charlotte had collapsed, nothing serious, she soon got up again, but she was hardly up to an evening's service and they were desperate for help. They must have been, they called me.

I cancelled dinner. It was my habit during my time editing the *AA Restaurant Guide* to work in the office all day and then take a train into London to eat. By 7.30 I'd usually be looking at a menu. Today was no exception, by 7.30 I had a menu in my hands and I didn't like the look of it.

That's not uncommon. I can really take a dislike to a menu. Not so much the content, important though that is, more the way in which they're sometimes written. Is there any other field in which so much flowery language is used to describe something that turns out to be so profoundly mediocre? Where, for instance, did *roquette* come from? Well, France obviously, but what's wrong with plain old rocket? What on earth is a *breath* of coulis? As for a *study* in anything, would you want to eat 'A Study in Celtic River Life'? Believe me, a few years ago I could have told you where to avoid it. Almost as annoying are the attempts to describe the association between ingredients on the plate, whether it's in terms of geography (since when did food go to sleep on a *bed* of anything?) or relationships (I once saw 'a *marriage* of chocolate fondant and a sweetened beetroot sauce' — a recipe for an early divorce if ever I've seen one). And these overwrought descriptions often come hand-in-hand with similarly elaborate script. Swirls and curls of frantic typeface adding a further layer of obscurity. The reality is that all this convoluted presentation adds up to one half of a pretty reliable equation. Let's call it the Law of Gastronomic

Relativity – an overcomplicated menu that misses the point equals overcomplicated food that misses the point. Not Einstein I know, but empirically true nevertheless.

This menu wasn't like that. The language was simple, understated even. I really liked the way it read. I just didn't want to cook it.

A good menu is not just written to be attractive to the customer, it's also written to reflect the capabilities of the kitchen. As it stood, the starters were eight in number and varied from the ultra-simple to the fairly tricky. Even on a busy night Charlotte could cope with it standing on her head (although not quite, evidently, lying on the floor). With me having been called off the bench, the balance between the difficulty of the menu and the capability of the kitchen had shifted violently and cried out to be redressed. I cut out the three most difficult dishes. There was still a choice of five but one of those was soup. I had a quick cigarette, scrubbed my hands, fastened my butcher's apron and thought of Marco. Bring it on.

The first table was six strong, a retirement party for a partner in a solicitor's practice. They arrived by taxi and it was soon clear that they hadn't come straight from the office. I knew most of them and they were pleased and surprised to see me back. They proffered a glass of Champagne – it would have been churlish to refuse. This was good news: not only did I know them, but they were too pissed to take too much notice of what they were eating. I returned to the kitchen with strengthened spirit.

The first check came in, a couple of smoked haddock tarts and one each of the other four dishes. I dealt with the hot starters first, then while they were cooking, moved on to the salads. Almost ready to go and another check came in, no problem, just get the other ones out first. I called the waitress and laid out the dishes on the pass with some pride, they looked pretty good to me. The kitchen is partly open to the restaurant and I watched the waitress make her way to the table with four of the plates. One of the lawyers gave a friendly wave, I gave a confident smile in return. Six down, twenty to go, this wasn't so difficult after all. The waitress returned, picked up the remaining plate and looked at me expectantly. I looked back at her, it seemed that she was waiting for something. One plate on the pass, four on the table, that made five starters. Five starters, six people, I'd missed a tart.

I could have cried. Suddenly there were two more checks in. I assembled the forgotten tart and stuck it in the oven. Next table, four goat's cheese. I put the cheese under the grill and turned to dressing the leaves. By the time I turned around again the cheese was on fire. At this point I started to swear, I blamed the grill, the heat was uncontrollable, how the hell could anyone work with that? Panic began to take its grip, the orders were piling up, I put more cheese on and that caught fire too, there wasn't much uncharred cheese left. Losing track of the orders, I sent dishes out to the wrong table. I was going down, sinking fast and doing my best to take the whole ship with me.

It was unforgivable. The one thing you don't do in the kitchen is panic. Panic is a luxury you can't afford, nothing but self-indulgence. Whatever happens you just have to keep going, take a breath, get your head in order, but keep doing the best you can, because the alternative is that the kitchen *goes down*.

Down is a word with a special resonance in restaurant kitchens. Down is a place where nobody wants to go. When a chef tells you, 'The kitchen went down last night,' it'll likely as not be accompanied by a wince. The kitchen going down is the equivalent of a stock-market crash or nuclear meltdown, it means a point of crisis has been reached where events are spiralling out of control, problems begin to accrue by the second and there seems no prospect of regaining mastery of events. When a kitchen goes down it's a hell of a fight to get it up again.

It can be sparked off by any number of things, a simple mistake, an awkward customer, anything that puts additional pressure on an operation that can rarely afford to have resources in reserve. If you're going to stay in business, you simply have to keep staff levels as close as possible to the minimum level necessary to run a service; if something happens to stretch those resources, the pressure comes on. If you have someone in the team that reacts to that pressure by blindly raging at kitchen appliances and wallowing in their own despair, you're in trouble. We were in trouble.

I've never been slapped in the face by a woman, but if ever I had such an assault due to me, it was then. This was my wife's kitchen, I was meant to be helping her but instead I was making matters worse. She's a gentle woman, tolerant, forgiving and not given to outbursts of anger. The pan hit the hotplate with enough force to stop me in mid-profanity. 'Right! You either calm down or you get out, because right now you're useless to me and if I have to do the starters as well then I bloody well will. Make your mind up.' It wasn't a slap in the face, but it stung just as hard.

Cowed, I slunk back to my corner of the kitchen and examined the checks. Working away steadily and now in silence, I gradually started to drag my head above water. The last couple of tables were late coming in and when their orders arrived I actually had time on my hands. By 9.30 I was finished.

As I made my way from the kitchen to the bar, one of the group of solicitors caught my arm. 'Hey, come and join us, have a drink, we haven't seen you for ages. That was a great meal. You know, Simon, it's not been quite the same since you left.' I sat down and let them pour me a glass of red. Rarely have I heard such nonsense and left it uncorrected.

EPILOGUE

Love and Money

She looked formidable. Not unlike Anne Widdecombe in her pre-poodle parlour days. Stout as a Russian Doll (the outer one), with a bullet-like bonnet of iron-grey hair, a plain blanket brown coat denied even the frivolity of a brooch and those sensible fur-lined boots you buy mail-order. As she approached the bar, bill in hand, I smiled determinedly but there was no response. Instead, she set her handbag down forcefully, snapped open the clasp and reached in for her purse. Her husband had already made for the exit – that would turn out to be a bad sign. Somewhere in the bar behind her a customer's phone rang. It was a simple gentle ring, like a landline but quieter, nothing elaborate or especially irritating and it was answered quickly. Considerately, the recipient walked outside to converse, but not before being reproached.

'Mobile phones are the worst thing man ever invented,' she declared in a voice without restraint.

I was tempted to argue. Other contenders came easily to mind. Nuclear, chemical and biological weapons, gas chambers, the thumbscrew, crack cocaine, slavery, private medicine, boy-bands, TV shows that begin 'The Hundred Best'…Christmas?

But I didn't, there seemed little point, after all, by now she had her purse out. She'd soon be on her way – but not yet.

'Now! I have something to tell you, something you really ought to know, for your own good.' Terrific, more valuable words of wisdom and me already deep in her debt for pointing out the evils of the mobile phone. She leant forward and delivered the news in an icy tone, a statement of fact, closed to argument; plain nasty, in fact.

'Your chef is utterly obsessed with garlic.'

Oh Jesus.

The chef (or one of them) happens to be my wife, if she has an obsession with garlic I've yet to detect it. Is there something this woman knows about my spouse that I don't? Has she spied her in the supermarket compulsively fondling those white tissued, purple-hearted heads whilst she thought nobody was looking. Maybe this woman runs a vegetable stall in town and my wife's been hanging around making herself a nuisance, caressing the bulbs, compulsively sniffing at the 'stinking rose'.

'I had the soup and all I could taste was garlic. As I said, your chef has an absolute obsession with garlic. That soup was *disgusting* …'

The way I look at it there's a line. I'll do all I can to keep the customer satisfied. This is because I like the customers and not just because they pay and keep us all a healthy distance from the benefits office. I really want them to be happy, I'll go a long way to make them feel at ease, I don't want them ever to feel awkward or intimidated or anything less than completely welcome and I'll try and ensure that's the case. If they don't like what we do, that's okay as well, they probably won't come twice. But like I said, there is a line and this woman vaulted across it with the use of that word – 'disgusting'.

'Stop … please. Don't call our food disgusting, the chef's my wife and she doesn't have a garlic obsession. As it happens I tasted the soup before lunch, you're right there is garlic but not much. If it had a fault, I think it was a touch under-seasoned but that might just be the fags. Either way, trust me, I know more about this than you do and I'd rather you …'

She interrupted, not to contradict me, as that would imply she was listening to what I had to say. '… And the beef! Never heard of anyone using garlic with roast beef. The meat was actually beautiful but quite spoilt by the garlic …'

At his point I realised there was little point in trying to hold up my end of the argument. The Widdie look-a-like was on transmit only and it occurred to me I could probably say anything to her, however foul and it wouldn't register. Believe me, I thought about it …

'… and I'm allergic to garlic.'

It's like you're trapped in some kind of Kafkaesque nightmare; there's no logic in what you're hearing and your own logic is a blunt instrument. You could scream but who'd hear you? She's allergic to garlic but she never thought to mention it. She's allergic to garlic but she's eaten the bloody food. She's allergic to garlic but, according to her, she's just consumed a tractor load of it and she's still standing in front of you, in rude, very rude, health. She's allergic to garlic, she's done nothing but complain and *she wants to book for next Wednesday.*

'We're full.'

'You're full?'

Of course not, six tables remained. I don't often turn away bookings – I'm too mercenary – but sometimes you have to be prepared to pay for your pleasures.

☆☆☆

It's not about the money though. Whenever you gather a few restaurateurs together, a clutch of those that have made it past the dangerous early year or two, where statistically most people hit the rocks, I can guarantee that at some point you'll hear the phrase 'you have to love it though, otherwise there's really no point'. And it's true, you really do have to love it. For the ten years that I was away from the trade I really missed it and, as the absence lengthened, the longing just grew. I yearned for the daily payback of people handing over some hard earned cash and bothering to thank you fulsomely on top of it, as if they had had the better part of the bargain. I was desperate to recapture the thrill of finding some gorgeous new ingredient for the kitchen to work with and to feel the pride of putting a new dish on the menu and watch it being delivered for the first time. I missed the warmth of encountering a new customer who shares your passion for food and treats the discovery of your restaurant with the wide-eyed excitement of a kid with an unexpected new toy. And most of all, I longed to tune in to the crackle of a full house, realising the room is ringing with the percussion, fizzing chatter and belly laughter that is the soundtrack to a great service. That sound can make your heart leap, just like love.

Of course, the problem with being in love is that you can get hurt. If you really care about the food you put out then an attack from the likes of the Widdie woman can be wounding. A couple of people pissed, mixing their drinks and throwing up when they get home then accusing you of poisoning them, that can upset you. Maybe you make a genuine mistake in the cooking of a steak and some shrieking woman decides to share her dissatisfaction with the entire dining room (usually after eating every morsel) that's deflating. But the money side of things isn't painful in that way, it's just a struggle, a mire you have to wade through on a daily basis trying to balance what you can you charge with what people are prepared to pay, whilst remaining conscious that you need to constantly top-up the flow of cash that streams out in the direction of suppliers, bureaucracy and the taxman. It's hard, especially if you really want to challenge your sanity and measure the returns in relation to the hours worked. As a financial enterprise it rarely makes much sense but that's exactly the point. You can't be wise and in love at the same time.

I'm not asking you to pity the poor restaurateur or even the poor chef. Quite obviously there are worse states of penury and some (although it's rare) make it pretty big. Gordon Ramsay is now a wealthy man. That much is obvious from his ever expanding (now global) network of restaurants, his high profile television exploits and the findings of the *Sunday Times* Rich List. He and Heston Blumenthal now have OBEs 'for services to the hospitality industry', Heston now also has a pub operation and his long dreamt of laboratory as well as a television presence. Shaun Hill is opening a new, much bigger restaurant in Worcester. In addition to his Michelin starred Petrus operation Marcus Wareing oversees the similarly celebrated Savoy Grill. But I don't for one minute think that they survived their apprenticeships on the distant promise of either riches or the prospect of gongs. The tales of those four chefs are illustrative and could easily be transposed for those of others of similar status but the theme wouldn't be any different. They were all captured by the same siren song, a love of good food, the desire to put it before the customer and a recognition of the pleasure that it brings.

Without exception, good restaurants are run by people that care with a passion about the food they serve. The fact that the majority of restaurants in Britain are not good largely reflects the fact that most of people involved in them, for one reason or another just don't care, or know how to care, about the food they offer. They couldn't give a toss and that's sometimes hard to stomach both for the customer and for those in the industry

I helped out on Ramsay's Channel 4 series, *Kitchen Nightmares*. The problems faced by the subject restaurants on Nightmares were diverse, but the first couple to be filmed were very much of the 'don't care' varietal. One lunch-time after the programme had been shot, I was in London at a meeting with the producer Christine Hall and Gordon Ramsay. Christine went off to the loo and Gordon leant across the table conspiratorially.

'It's not really like this Simon is it?'

'Like what?'

'Like these places we've seen. They're the extreme end right?'

He was genuinely taken aback at what he'd seen. It struck me that the vast majority of his cooking life, with the exception of his very first job had been spent in high quality kitchens. Largely he'd been insulated from this part of the market and I think it had taken him somewhat by surprise. Were these places the extreme end? Not really. I'd seen plenty that would give them a run for the money in their capacity to appal. For Gordon Ramsay being introduced to these places with their shoddy practices, lack of basic understanding and young head chefs who seemed to think that lumping any old crap into a ring mould in the centre of an unfeasibly large plate and squirting some balsamic circles around it was the way to impress the punters was a bit of an eye-opener. By the second series he was a little less easy to shock.

The trouble is, it's still much easier to eat out badly in the UK than to eat out well. If you were to take a random journey across Britain choosing restaurants at the shake of a dice and deprived of any assistance from guide books, you'd seldom get lucky. Candidates for *Ramsay's Kitchen Nightmares* weren't thin on the ground. The problem instead was to avoid telling the same story every week. Namely, the chef can't cook, he's as lazy as a Jif lemon and his kitchen's a cesspit. People sometimes ask how on earth, knowing they are going to be filmed would anyone leave their kitchen in such a nauseating state? Well believe it or not, it's often because they don't recognise the squalor that surrounds them. It's like when I was a teenager and my mother would complain, justifiably, about the post-apocalypse state of my bedroom. I'd take a look around at the abandoned clothes, scattered magazines, empty glasses and dirty coffee mugs before telling her honestly that I genuinely couldn't see what the problem was. Before filming one of the episodes I went to visit a candidate restaurant where I chatted to the chef-owner for an hour or so front of house before I eventually asked to see the kitchen. As he got up to show me through he hesitated. 'Ah, now here's one thing I'm not worried about if Gordon comes,' he said. 'I can't be criticised for a lack of cleanliness. My kitchen's always spotless.'

I followed him in, there was debris everywhere. For half a second I expected him to cry out that whilst we'd been in the restaurant somebody had broken in and ransacked the kitchen, but no, that bread roll poking out from under the fridge wasn't a new arrival – bread doesn't turn that colour without the benefit of time.

Things have changed, and for the better. Early in this book I talked about the wonder of eating out in London these days. Look there and you can be elated, look further afield and there's so much less to get excited about. Of course, there are good places to eat outside of the capital, but they are scattered – limited to the sporadic ploughing of lonely furrows in the countryside and the occasional bright sparks in city centres.

I keep saying it's not about the money, but that's part of the problem. The fact that you can go and eat decently outside of the capital is largely down to the enthusiasm of the mad buggers who keep those pubs, small hotels and restaurants going. If they're good, these places tend to be pretty busy by virtue of rarity value and it's easy to get the impression that whoever owns the place is coining it. I guarantee you they're not. If they're lucky they're making a reasonable living by working unreasonable hours. This is fine for those prepared to put up with it but it's hardly an incentive for others to do the same.

How much would you pay for a good meal? £30? £60? £90? It depends, I suppose, on what you mean by good. A few years back I recall paying around £150 to eat at the then three Michelin Star Oak Room under Marco Pierre White. The bill included a third share in a bottle and a half of decent but not extravagant wine and perhaps a gin and tonic. We were there for around three hours, so our evening's entertainment set us back £50 an hour. Was it worth it? Naturally – it was amongst the best meals I have ever had, I can still remember the detail (a rarity in itself) and I still think of it as some of the best money I ever spent.

Also fresh in my mind is the reaction of one or two acquaintances when I happened to mention the cost soon afterwards. Understandably there was some incredulity that I'd been 'daft' enough to shell out that kind of cash for a single meal. Was it really that good? Could any three courses really be worth that kind of money? Sometimes it strikes me that there's something odd about the way we perceive value for money in restaurants. How much would it cost for instance to have three courses and a similar quantity of booze in some pub chain restaurant? Around £30 would be a reasonable guess, perhaps a little more. So that begs the comparison – was dinner at the Oak Room five times as good? Well clearly the answer is no. Measured on quality it was almost infinitely better. Where would I be more likely to feel ripped off? Not at the Oak Room.

The Oak Room (now a venue for afternoon teas) is an extreme example. Most really good food costs nothing like that amount and as a consequence is even closer to the price of the really bad stuff. In fact, in many cases, the *price of good food is pretty much the same as the price of bad food* which is something of an oddity when you think about it. In most other cases you get what you pay for. You buy a bargain basement music system that does the job you pay one price, but if you're really into that stuff you buy something of much better quality at a much higher price. For some reason that equation that seems to be accepted by the public in so many areas doesn't seem to fully apply to eating out – people are prepared to pay a little bit more, but not much.

And yet we seem prepared to be ripped off on a daily basis and most often it's by the chains that ply their miserable trade in our shopping centres, multiple 'inns' and motorway service stations. The latter, are I know, a common target for scorn and every now and then they seem to respond with a risible pretence that they're making a new effort, usually by way of some celebrity chef endorsement or other. Maybe it's because it's still fresh in my mind, perhaps it's because I've been rather spoilt in recent years and have lost touch with the reality of everyday eating out in Britain, but I'm pretty convinced that a short while ago, fetching my son back from university in Nottingham (naturally he was on the point of starvation), I had an experience at a motorway service station that set a new benchmark for awful restaurant food. In many ways this was a quite remarkable meal in that it had absolutely no redeeming features. In fact, it was so extraordinarily miserable that I feel inclined to share it with you, blow by depressing blow.

Service (and I'm not sure you can credibly call it that) – hopelessly slow, grudging and lacking even the faintest whiff of hospitality. Not that the staff can really be blamed, they were clearly understaffed, harassed and no doubt embarrassed about the muck they were serving up.

Quality (it was fish and chips by the way) – abysmal, barely lukewarm, batter with the texture of a used sponge and a handful of chips whose every wrinkle spoke of advancing years and inhumane treatment.

Presentation – well good food tends to look good, bad food bad, so I don't need to paint you a picture do I? Suffice to say that this dish looked at its most appealing when covered by an opaque plastic dome designed, rather hopefully, to keep the heat in.

Value for Money – Two of these, with a couple of coffees, set me back nearly twenty quid. Even taking into account the fact that the coffee was hot, they provided us with seats and threw in free use of the toilet facilities, I felt like I'd been mugged.

Sympathy of course, is not in order. I really should have known better than to go there in the first place and it had been many years since I'd done so. It was a useful reminder though there really is no valid reason for food to be this bad but, of course, it will be if those providing it think they can get away with it. It costs more to do things properly, so if these places can avoid that alternative (say if they have a fairly captive market), they will.

Pick up a broadsheet in the early months of the year and the chances are that shouting at you from the top will be something along the lines of 'EAT OUT FOR A FIVER'. Two courses for five pounds, you can't argue with that can you? Well I can as it happens. These are the same papers that in their food pages extol the virtues of high quality ingredients, locally produced food and seasonality. Yet they are promoting the idea that you can fund the ingredients for a couple of courses, the chef's time to cook them, the waiting staff to deliver them, the heat, the light, all the overheads and almost a quid of VAT from a fiver and make a profit. True they might have a drink or two (although my experience is that the lunch for a fiver brigade don't tend to attack the high end clarets) and it's a quiet time of the year when it's nice to have some trade, however unprofitable.

But it's an awful message to send out. If they can do it for a fiver now, why can't they do that all the time? If restaurant X can do it why can't restaurant Y? Or worse, restaurant Y feels obliged to do it because restaurant X down the road is signed-up. Ironically, when this all started over fifteen years ago in the *FT* it was a really good idea. Two courses for a fiver was at least a little more realistic then. Nicholas Lander, whose innovation it was, selected a limited number of restaurants on the basis of quality (with reference to the *Good Food Guide*, I think) and it operated as something of a reward to places that were trying that bit harder to offer decent food. Now it just seems like an obsession with trying to drive the price down – the same papers that bemoan the quality of eating out outside of London are making a handy contribution to making any improvement near impossible. The deal should be that the customer expects to get good food at a reasonable price. Good food at a bargain price is a nice idea but it's an illusion, unsustainable and putting that idea in people's heads is well ... unhelpful.

211

$$\star\,\star\,\star$$

'Hi, booked a table of ten but there's only six of us, four couldn't make it.'

That's a downer. Four is one tenth of the total covers, probably about £150 gross. It's Saturday night, we could have sold that table a dozen times today alone. This probably means we won't hit our weekly target. It's a shame but it happens, no point in making them feel awkward about it.

'No bother. Let us get you some drinks and I'll bring over the menus.'

Ten minutes later the same guy approaches the bar.

'So it's £25.50 for three courses right?'

'That's it.'

'What if we don't want three courses?'

'It's still £25.50. That's our price on Fridays and Saturdays.'

'Okay. Just wanted to check,' and he wanders back to his smaller then expected party.

There's no reason why I should feel awkward about this but I do. The two evenings we can guarantee being full are Friday and Saturday and we simply can't afford for people to occupy a table for the evening and spend the price of a main course alone. So it's £25.50 for three courses, take it or leave it. Sometimes people can't manage a dessert so we package it up for them and they take it away. That feels better, at least they've had what they paid for.

212

Another five minute pass, I'm just about to go over and take the order but he's already on his way over.

'Is it alright if I cancel the table?'

It's 8.30 on a Saturday night. We're in the middle of the country-side. We don't get people calling in on spec for a meal at this time of night. Somehow the word cancel doesn't seem appropriate.

'Why would you want to do that?'

'We don't all want three courses.'

This is tongue-chewing time. I truly want to tell the guy to get lost and never even think about trying to book again. On the other hand we've already lost the revenue from the four that stood him up, to extend that to ten is just too depressing.

I try not to sound too exasperated. 'I'll be honest with you. I'd rather you stayed and just pay for the courses you have. You've gone from ten and to six that's a significant loss in a forty-seater restaurant on a Saturday night. If the rest of you go we may as well not have opened ... stay, just pay for what you order.'

They did, mostly taking only one course and a single drink. When he came to pay the party leader was full of praise for the food.

'... and I'm really sorry about, y'know.'

'No worries, that's fine, you'll know next time.' I can't hold a grudge for long and he seemed to have got the point.

'... and this is for the staff.'

Two quid – fair play to the man.

Reading these passages back, I get the feeling they might come across as a little miserly. I need you to know that I'm actually a generous soul by nature; I buy the odd drink for the regulars and I'm not against the occasional special offer either. In fact here's one; bring in a copy of this book and if I'm there I'll buy you a glass of wine (terms and conditions apply).

☆ ☆ ☆

The tales in this book are extraordinary only in a relative sense. Nothing here compares in fortitude terms to the hitchhiking chef I picked up by chance in South Africa, cutting his usual walk to and from work of seventeen kilometres each way by half. There are many more demanding jobs in this country too, of course, certainly less satisfying ones and there's no doubt that many derive some intrinsic reward from the 'swagger' that accrues to those who stand-up to the particular physical and mental challenges of the kitchen, but there's not much doubt either that the prime motivator, even amongst the posturing, is the ardour for good food and it's chiefly that desire that feeds the devotion.

Shaun Hill, Marcus Wareing, Gordon Ramsay, Heston Blumenthal – whatever their motivations, the net effect of their labours and many others of their ilk, is that Britain has become a better place to eat out and that's something that needs to be recognised, celebrated and most of all, nurtured.

Because mostly, it's still bloody awful, and it would be so good to see that change.

ACKNOWLEDGEMENTS

Thanks must go to the Tough Cookies for such generosity with their precious time, to Maryann, Joe, Jamie and my parents Tony and Anita for their unshakeable belief, their tolerance and their love and to my big friend Mark Manson for his sideways thoughts and constant encouragement.

And special thanks to Martin Morgan – in many ways a 'normal guy' and in every way an inspiration.